A Grassroots History of the American Civil War

Volume II
The Bully Seventh Ohio Volunteer Infantry

Richard J. Staats

HERITAGE BOOKS
2009

HERITAGE BOOKS
AN IMPRINT OF HERITAGE BOOKS, INC.

Books, CDs, and more—Worldwide

For our listing of thousands of titles see our website
at
www.HeritageBooks.com

Published 2009 by
HERITAGE BOOKS, INC.
Publishing Division
100 Railroad Ave. #104
Westminster, Maryland 21157

Copyright © 2003 Richard J. Staats

All rights reserved. No part of this book may be reproduced or transmitted in any form or by any means, electronic or mechanical, including photocopying, recording or by any information storage and retrieval system without written permission from the author, except for the inclusion of brief quotations in a review.

International Standard Book Numbers
Paperbound: 978-0-7884-2374-1
Clothbound: 978-0-7884-8088-1

CONTENTS

Introduction: v

Chapter One: "seeking whom they might devour"....................... 1
    Camp Dennison, Campaigning in Western Virginia.

Chapter Two: "something to be a soldier in winter" 29
    Winter Campaigning, 1861-1862.

Chapter Three: "I saw enough of the horrors of war" 45
    The Shenandoah Campaign, 1862.

Chapter Four: "like grass before the mower" 69
    From Winchester to Antietam.

Chapter Five: "The spring of 1863 beholds us in belligerent
    attitude" 99
    Chancellorsville, Gettysburg, and the Home Front

Chapter Six: "Let us have the 7th back" 123
    Chattanooga and Ringgold

Chapter Seven: "An outburst of exultation rent the air" 135
    The Atlanta Campaign

Chapter Eight: "So teach us to number our days" 155
    The Aftermath.

Footnotes: 169

Bibliography: 177

Index: 179

INTRODUCTION

Serenity and the promises of springtime permeated the misty fresh air in the Little Miami River valley. The soggy fields, where corn, wheat, and vegetable gardens had abundantly flourished in the summer of 1860, now awaited the industrious plowman and planter. On the steep hillside that hemmed in the rushing river and bottom land, bright green tree leaf buds brilliantly speckled the landscape. Red breasted robins and a multitude of their avian cousins cast an eye to the fallow ground, performed some hasty pecking, and then flitted off to their new nests. Around the scattered German houses, daffodils and tulips raised their colorful heads as an object lesson to the Resurrection during this Easter season. Throughout the valley, quiet and peace reigned supreme in this April of 1861.

Ominous war clouds preempted nature's normal routine in the valley; and the tranquillity suddenly vanished as a host of bustling, energetic men swarmed to this idyllic spot seventeen miles northeast of Cincinnati. By mid-May the population in the valley surpassed that of the largest cities in the State of Ohio.

The "Iron Horse" was the chief offender to the solitude in the valley. The chuffing steam engine, shrill whistle, and clacking wheels ushered in a horde of eager, excited, and babbling Union volunteers. Eventually, the "cars," as the train was called, carted them off to the "front," which seemed to be some vague, mystical place. Shouted commands, halloos, and equally loud responses came from the throats of 30,000 would-be soldiers. Laughter and music frequently punctuated the cacophony. Horses, mules, wagons, and the footsteps of thousands of humans churned up the springtime mud, and the April showers added to the quagmire. The staccato ring of axes and hammers beat a steady tattoo as huts were constructed for the volunteers. Hovering over the valley was an acrid layer of smoke, which caused watering eyes, nagging coughs, and a constant clearing of throats. Often, these physical responses masked the symptoms of the widepread common colds, pneumonia, measles, and other potentially fatal diseases. This was Camp Dennison.

Among the throng in Camp Dennison were the Tyler Guards and the Franklin Rifles who would always occupy a special place in the hearts of the people in Portage County, Ohio. Like parents who are fond of all of their children, yet have special memories of the first born, the citizenry deeply revered their first volunteers to fight in the War of the Rebellion. The Franklin Rifles and the Tyler Guards were the first two local companies to be raised in response to President Lincoln's first call for 75,000 volunteers to put down the rebellion. In April 1861 each company received a grand, patriotic, and emotional send-off by the home folks. Now, in June 1861 the two Portage County companies were part of the Seventh Ohio Volunteer Infantry. The Franklin Rifles were primarily from the Franklin Township area. Franklin Mills, modern day Kent, Ohio, was the center of the township. The Tyler Guards were centered on Ravenna, the county seat, but some of the volunteers hailed from nearby townships. In time their fanciful names were replaced by the standard military lettering of companies. The Franklin Rifles became Company F, and the Tyler Guards became Company G in the 7th Ohio Volunteer Infantry.

Both companies passed through the three months' volunteer stage of the war in Camp Taylor at Cleveland and at Camp Dennison. Those volunteers who re-enlisted for the three years' service enjoyed a furlough back home. Now, they were eager for the fray, all 1,020 men of the 7th Ohio Volunteer Infantry. The "boys" were also eager to inform the people back home of their continued commitment to the cause, and the best way to spread the word was to write to the local newspapers, which were more than happy to fill their pages with news from the local soldiers. The most prolific writing came from former employees of the newspapers; however, friends and relatives of the soldiers also contributed their soldier letters to the newspapers.

After a pleasant furlough the boys returned to the squalid conditions of Camp Dennison. With the effervescence and optimism of youth, they were undaunted by their present condition or the future. All of the boys were absolutely sure that the Union was going to prevail once they met the foe south of the Ohio River. If for no other reason, it was because they were "in the right." Most of the boys were absolutely sure that they would return home to Portage County, and that the triumphant journey would be quite soon. None of the boys believed the obnoxious canard that one southron could whip five or more Yankees, and the 7th Ohio was eager to prove the lie. If there were any nagging doubts as to how they would perform under the booming cannons and rattling musketry, they were going to keep it a private matter. The possibility that any of them would become hardened killers, disillusioned and jaded warriors, or horribly maimed in body and spirit was unthinkable. In June 1861, who would not go for a soldier?

Chapter One

"seeking whom they might devour"

Camp Dennison,
June 20, '61

Eds. Democrat:

Having provided myself with a cheese box for a writing desk, and being blessed with the stillness attending a "grand walk around" dance in the barracks, in which there are not over fifty participants, each endeavoring to outdo the rest in the way of noise. I proceed to drop a few lines to your paper, relative to matters and things at Camp Dennison.

During last night and this morning, we enjoyed quite a refreshing shower of rain, which has left the parade grounds in an excellent condition for drilling, and many of the companies are out taking advantage of this rare opportunity of going through their maneuvers without being suffocated.

FULL COMPANIES

The companies composing the 7th Regiment are all full, and were yesterday and to day mustered in for three years service, by Capt. Howard, of the 4th Regiment of Artillery from Cincinnati.

All the three months men who declined going for the war, have left camp on furlough for their respective homes, where they will remain subject to the call of the government, until the expiration of their term of enlistment.

9TH REGIMENT

The 9th Regiment (German) under command of Col. G. W. McCook, left camp on Monday last for some point in Virginia. They are a fine body of men and go into the field well armed and equipped.

INSPECTION OF THE 7TH

On Tuesday afternoon the arms of the 7th Regiment were inspected by Maj. Gen. McClellan, and the muskets now in use condemned. The General highly complimented the 7th upon their appearance and drill pronouncing it the best regiment on the ground, and assured Col. Tyler that we should in a few days be fully armed and equipped, ready for the march at a moment's warning.

INDIANA TROOPS

The 6th and 7th Indiana regiments passed through the camp this morning en route to Washington. They all seemed to be well provided with every essential article of warfare.

QUELLING A RIOT

About nine o'clock Monday last, while many of the soldiers were engaged in writing, others in reading, and still others whose literary talents had perhaps never been largely cultivated, had quietly laid themselves down upon the soft side of a board to rest their weary limbs after the fatiguing drills of the day, the war cry, To arms! To arms! caused every man to leap to his feet, seize a musket, and fall into ranks. The regiment was formed in an almost incredible short space of time, and were on the march, "seeking whom they might devour," headed by the band playing Yankee Doodle. – Some excitement existing in the ranks, Col. Tyler's voice was heard, clear and distinct as bugle notes: "Keep cool men, I want you to charge. Commandants of companies will see that there is no talking in the ranks" – and away we went on the "double quick" for the supposed scene of conflict; but ere we reached it, we were commanded to halt by the Colonel, who had ridden ahead of us and learned the condition of affairs there. He said, "Men, we have been called out to-night to quell a riot between two regiments on the opposite side of the Railroad; that has been accomplished without our aid and you can now march back to your quarters." Before dismissing the regiment, however, the Colonel highly complimented the men upon their promptness in turning out, and expressed the hope that they might even manifest the same disposition to promptly respond to duty's call. The riot was between soldiers of the 10th and 13th regiments, and grew out of the shooting of one of the former's men by a guard of the latter while endeavoring to cross one of the regimental lines. Several shots were fired, and some six or eight wounded, but as I understand, no one killed.

REGIMENTAL ELECTION

The 7th regiment held its election for field officers for the three years service on Wednesday last, which resulted in the election of the old officers by a unanimous vote. E. B. Tyler, Colonel; W. R. Creighton, Lieut. Colonel; J. C. Casemate, Major. These are the men whom the 7th Regiment have chosen to fight under in defense of the glorious Stars and Stripes. During their past official career, they have won the confidence and respect of every man in the ranks.

CAPT. STEDMAN RESIGNS

Mr. William Stedman has resigned his position as Captain of the Franklin Rifle Company and Mr. D. B. Clayton of the Cleveland Light Guards has been chosen in his place.

MARCHING ORDERS

The 3rd and 4th Regiments have received their arms and equipments and have orders to leave camp on Saturday for Western Virginia.

Col. Tyler expects to receive marching orders for the 7th Regiment in less than twenty-four hours. Our destination will also be Virginia.

Hoping that my next may be dated from some point in Virginia, I will close by submitting myself

Very respectfully, D. G. S. [1]

[D. G. S. was 22 year old Pvt. David G. Stein of Company A.]

The following letter from Camp Dennison was described by the editor as being from a friend on the staff of Col. Tyler. It was dated June 23, 1861. The "friend" exuded a confidence and pride in the regiment that bordered on cockiness.

> We have done a large amount of business to day, not with- standing it is Sunday – viz: distributed 200 Enfield Rifles and 800 first rate U. S. muskets, and 1,000 each of knapsacks, haversacks and bayonet scabbards to our men, and will have 1,000 canteens to give them to-morrow. It made the boys "laugh all over" when they were ordered to march to the Depot Quarter Master's and leave their old muskets, (bearing date 1823) and return to our Headquarters and receive a splendid gun and bayonet in place of them. They were so impatient to get hold of a good gun that we had to post a guard around them to keep them away long enough to fix the bayonets on them and count them out.
>
> It looks very much like leaving these "diggins" at short notice, as we received 10,000 rounds of rifle cartridges today, and also a lot of camp equipage. I should not be surprised we were in Virginia quite as soon as this letter is in

your town. We have a fine set of men and they drill very well indeed, taking into consideration the number of raw recruits lately enlisted.

Gen. Cox has received his appointment from Washington as Commander of the 2nd Brigade and will probably move with the 7th Regiment, and I am glad of it, as he is a gentleman in every respect, "or any other man."

Everything has gone on very smoothly and quietly at Camp since the *three months grumblers were sent home*, and the accounts of starvation and other calamities at Camp Dennison are not published any more by the press. I suppose their correspondents have gone home on furlough to remain until mustered out of service. [2]

The Seventh Regiment finally received its opportunity to cross the Ohio River and to enter the land of secession and slavery. It is interesting to note the low opinion held for the people of Western Virginia in the beginning of the following letter and the enlightened opinion at the end in describing how the citizens provided the soldiers with abundant food and treats.

Head Quarters 7th Regiment O. V.
"Camp Taylor," Weston, Va., July 4, 1861

We left Camp Dennison last Wednesday night and arrived at Bellaire the next day at 11:30 a.m., and crossed the Ohio River to Benwood, Virginia directly opposite, and in appearance it is certainly fifty years behind the town on the Ohio side of the river, and it is as God forsaken a place as any one I ever saw. We left for Grafton on the Ohio and Baltimore R. R. at 2 a.m. on Friday morning on a lot of freight cars – and as we expected to be attacked at any moment our men had their guns loaded and plenty of ball and cartridges in their boxes. We heard of war, secessionists, troops fired on, etc., a few miles ahead; and after reaching that point, inquired, and it was like the "milk sickness" about five miles further on. The country and the people look just alike – a barren, hilly country, and the people look all alike, of a dirty brown color, ragged and dirty, and may justly be termed as they are, the "white trash" – mostly Irish at that. We arrived at Grafton at noon, where we saw the smiling face of our Colonel, and

Looking down Culp's Hill. The Confederates attacked from the left of the picture. Photo by the author.

he was greeted by hearty cheers. The country in and about Grafton looks more like a place to live in than any we passed through since leaving the glorious old State of Ohio, and it improves as we get towards Clarksburg where we proceeded at once after getting our Colonel on board the train. We passed thro' a number of long tunnels, some of which were three-fourths of a mile through, and if the Railroad had not been guarded by Union troops, I'm thinking the rebels would have sent some of us to the "happy land of Canaan" in passing through the tunnels and deep cuts in the mountains. We pitched our tents and had one night's rest, (the first since leaving Camp Dennison) and the next day (Saturday) at 4 p.m. we started on a forced march for Weston, a distance of twenty-three miles over a mountainous country, and very thinly settled, and it was very hard on our men, as it was extremely hot and they had not recovered from the fatigue of the Railroad journey – they would sit down by the side of the road and say, I cannot go any further; but by encouraging some and putting others on the baggage wagons, we succeeded in getting them into town where we arrived about 4 a.m. on Sunday morning. The rebels had made their arrangement to take the town on Sunday, and as we neared the bridge going into town, our advanced guard discovered a man on the lookout who appeared to be one of their pickets, and when ordered to halt, he run and was fired on by our men, and like "Davy Crockett's coon, he concluded to come down," as he said our men fired a little too close for comfort or safety, as he could feel the balls singe his hair, although he was about 800 yards off and running at the time they fired.

  We took possession of the town by flanking the outskirts, the main body marching up the principal street, taking possession of the Bank and public buildings, and arresting about twenty secessionists. The principal men or leaders were sent to Grafton, and the others were allowed to go at large after taking the oath of allegiance to the Government.

  There were $30,000 in coin in the Bank here belonging to the State, which was forwarded to Wheeling to the loyal Government to keep it out of the hands of the rebels, as most of the office holders are of that stripe.

  The people were almost dead with fear, when they heard our band playing up the street. They thought the rebel army had them sure; but when they saw the Colonel, their joy was excessive. They are raising poles and spreading the stars and stripes to the breeze, and ladies are coming out with aprons made of the glorious banner.

Today our camp has been full of men, women, and children from the country, and our boys have had a glorious time, as the people furnished them with turkeys, chickens, hams, bread, pies, cakes, etc., etc., enough for two days rations. They think the Ohio boys are their preservers.

I believe the Colonel knows every person in this country [Prior to the war Col. Tyler had a business in that area for a fur company.], as they come a distance of forty miles to see him, and all want him to send men to their towns, as they are afraid to stay on account of the scoundrels who are driving them from their homes and stealing their property; but as soon as they hear of troops coming the cowardly scoundrels run, but if our boys ever get a chance at them, they will have a mortality list that will keep them in mind of the 7th Ohio.[3]

The following letter by "Everett" shows his aversion to marching long distances for no apparent reason. Although he is now permitted to forage from the secessionists, he has second thoughts about the rightness of that practice. Everett is associated with Company F, but the name is apparently a pseudonym.

Camp near Glenville, Va.
Thursday, July 11, 1861

...On Sunday, the 7th Companies H and B under the command of Capt. Asper of Warren, were detailed to visit Glenville, distance 28 miles from Weston, and attend to the rebels in that place. In the Evening, Capt. Asper sent back for re-enforcements. Reliable reports also came in that the rebels had collected to the number of fifteen hundred and were continually increasing, with the intention of crushing out the Union troops in that place. Monday morning the 7th, with the exception of Company A, started for the scene of action, every one in good spirits at the prospects of a brush. It was very hot during the fore part of the day, and a heavy thunder shower in the afternoon conspired to make the march disagreeable, and when after getting 20 miles of the distance, we were ordered to halt, and were told that the rebels had again fled, the curses of the tired men were both loud and deep. We immediately encamped for the night and pursued our way the next day, finding the rebels as usual *not there*, reports saying that they had retreated some ten or fifteen miles for cannon and reenforcements. It was confidently asserted that we would be attacked today but I am now writing by candle light and have not heard even a picket gun for the last four hours. We shall probably march again soon, where to it is the privilege of the common soldier not to know. Since coming to Glenville, we have had the privilege of foraging from the *secesh*. It looks bad to see the property of these persons so confiscated, and though we have the permission of our officers, I cannot persuade myself that it is right. Company F has got hold of a barrel of Sorghum molasses, and as long as it lasts, I think we shall have light consciences. Government furnishes us no meat in this place, and for the past day or two no bread – as a natural consequence, secesh beef, mutton, fowl, and flour have suffered. The health of the camp is as good as can be expected under the circumstances. Company F has suffered the most I think, having at one time sixteen representatives in the hospital. We are now, however, getting toughened to it, and begin to feel healthy and strong again.

EVERETT [4]

Camp of the 7th regiment
Near Bulltown, Va.,
Friday, July 26, 1861

Eds. Democrat:

PREPARING FOR THE ENEMY

I think I wrote you last from Glenville. For a portion of the time there we lay expecting an attack every night. One night about two o'clock we were quickly roused and formed into line for the purpose of receiving another allowance of cartridges. We were then ordered to lie with our equipments on and sleep with "One eye open," ready for any emergency. All of this preparation was caused by the reception of a message soon after midnight stating that the rebels were within ten or fifteen miles marching upon us. But this, like many other messages, proved to be without foundation.

SHOOTING

Corporal Adams of Company C was shot one morning while on picket guard. The wound is not dangerous, being a mere flesh wound on the left side. Capt. Shurtliff of the same Company was also shot at the same day in nearly the same place, the ball taking effect in his horse, wounding it so as to make it perfectly useless.

MARCHING AFTER A RUNNING ENEMY

We lay in Glenville until last Saturday afternoon when we received orders to prepare for a march. At Seven P. M. we started taking the turnpike leading toward Bulltown. We marched until one A. M. when we turned into a field, and each man rolling himself up in his blanket, slept soundly until morning. We carried our rations in our haversacks, consequently breakfast was a short affair. A little coffee or tea was made, which with our crackers and cold beef was quite palatable. To finish with, we went up on a hill and regaled ourselves with blackberries, which we find in the greatest profusion on the hills of the "Old Dominion." The line of march was taken up at about eight o'clock, proceeding steadily along for about six miles when the column was halted, and we were told that we should probably meet the rebels within the next two or three miles. This news seemed only to increase the enthusiasm of the men, who bore with considerable impatience the long halt there occasioned. At about one P. M. we started forward, moving slowly and cautiously, expecting to meet something. We kept going until sundown, when we met the 17th and 13th regiments together with Companies A and D of the 7th at Bulltown.

PAINESVILLE BAND

Here we met the Painesville Band, Prof. Eileman, late of Garrettsville [Portage County], leader, which I think augurs favorably for some good music.

IN THE KANAWHA

We pitched our tents, got a good supper, and slept well during the night. Reveille roused the men as usual the next morning, and a more beautiful morning I had not seen in Virginia. The fore part of the day was spent by the soldiers bathing in the Kanawha, the water of which was the purest here of any place that I have found.

AFTER THE ENEMY AGAIN

In the afternoon we started to meet a force of rebels on the Jacksonville turnpike who were retreating before the advance of Gen. McClellan and were supposed to be about ten miles distant. We felt jubilant for we were sure that we had got them at last. We marched about six miles, turned into a wheat field, and encamped. We are here yet. Company A has taken about half the wagons and gone out foraging. Reports say that the rebels have got away, but I sooner think that it is the intention to surround them and keep them enclosed until they are forced to submit.[5]

The next two letters to the newspaper were written on Sunday, August 4, 1861. There is little duplication, which is probably due to the different personalities and duties of the correspondents, "Everett" of Company F and "D. H. W." of Company G. The latter is 21 year old Cpl. Daniel H. Wright.

Camp 7th Reg't, Beyond Sutton ...
To-day seems the most like a Sabbath of any we have spent in Virginia, owing to the fact that we have been very busy most of the time, and for some reason especially as on the Sabbath until this time. But to-day we are allowed to rest.

We entered Sutton one week ago to-day, having had a disagreeable march through the rain, it being noticeable that with one or two exceptions the Seventh Regiment has not entered camp but in rain. There were with us two pieces of light artillery, three howitzers manned by regulars, some of whom have seen upwards of twenty years service, and the Seventeenth and Thirteenth Ohio Regiments, the whole under the immediate command of Col. Tyler. A Company of Virginia "Snake Hunters" also came with us, they being sort of a guerrilla organization and proving very valuable as scouts. They enjoy considerable local celebrity, and a more wild and hardy set of individuals I have ever seen. They are here, there, and everywhere, almost in the same time. They were with us, in all, about a week and have now left to search for new adventures elsewhere.

We remained in Sutton for four days at work digging rifle pits, throwing up breastworks, and otherwise fortifying the place, thereby preparing to give the "Wise Brigade" [Confederate forces in the area] a flattering reception if it should see fit to visit us. But "it" didn't see fit to pay us the visit; so on the first of August, the whole force, with the exception of the Seventeenth [Regt.] took up the line of march, moving South in quest of adventure. It was by all odds the warmest day we have experienced in the Old Dominion. Government has not furnished us with canteens, and for a considerable distance over the mountains no water could be obtained; yet scarcely any murmurs were heard. But when we did reach water, a good many of the poor fellows drank so much that they were unable to proceed further. We marched very slow, halting frequently to rest. The column was halted and tents pitched at an early hour, thus giving man and beast time to refresh themselves – We started early the next morning and proceeded to our present camping ground.

We are now traveling through a country of beautiful scenery, but like all mountainous regions, barren and unprofitable. Occasionally we descend into a little valley through which runs a small stream of the best water, and which a settler finds room to raise his log cabin, plant a garden, and perhaps a small piece of corn, and he manages to live somehow.

We are to march again to-morrow morning at four o'clock. I will try and write you again soon.

Everett [6]

The following, designed for the Sentinel, but too late to appear in that paper, has been handed to the Democrat for publication:

Birch Mountain, Nicholas Co., Va. ...

Editor Sentinel: We the Scouting Regiment, or Seventh Ohio, are now encamped in the valley between the two ridges of Big Birch mountain, where a day or two since, were encamped Wise's Brigade, or at least a part of it, as we found boxes marked "Wise's Brigade" in the deserted camp when we arrived here yesterday noon.

When last I wrote you on Friday [of last] week, we were encamped a few miles north of Sutton, in a large wheat field I believe. On Saturday, the 27th ult., at 4 o'clock in the afternoon, Col. Tyler gave us orders to march, which we quickly obeyed, glad to get out of this extensive mud-hole. Just at twilight, we arrived at what is called Flatwoods, where the shabby remains of a Secesh camp were dimly seen. We here pitched our tents for the night. A letter to the commanding officer of the rebel force was found upon the ground by one of our troops, instructing him, should the enemy (meaning us) prove too strong, to retreat to Sutton, and from there, should he deem it necessary, he might retreat to Birch mountain, where we now are, and there make a bold stand, but they very unceremoniously left it before we arrived here!

On Sunday afternoon, at ten o'clock, we left the Flatwoods

for Sutton. The day was very warm and water scarce, and as our regiment are not as yet provided with canteens, the troops suffered much for want of water. At three o'clock in the afternoon we arrived at Sutton, the county-seat of Braxton county, which is pleasantly situated on the north bank of the elk river. After halting for some time in the street to rest, our band the while discoursing sweet music, we were marched to the top of a hill north of the town where we pitched our tents. While going up the hill, Sergeant Lecompte of Co. A fell dead in the ranks, of palpitation of the heart. His body was interred with military honors on Monday forenoon in a retired portion of the camp, Rev. Mr. Drake of Lexington, Perry county, Ohio officiating in the absence of our Chaplain, Rev. Mr. Brown.

Elk river at Sutton is spanned by a beautiful wire suspension bridge three hundred and sixty feet in length. The waters of Elk river are cool, deep and clear, and afforded a grand sporting place for our troops while at that place. We were at Sutton five days, meanwhile strongly fortifying our camp by digging several rifle pits and throwing up strong fortifications behind which were planted our battery. Co. G went out with muskets, axes, picks and spades about two miles up the mountain to the south of camp where they built a strong picket guard post. We were two days in perfecting the station Tuesday and Wednesday working as we never worked before. Col. Tyler was with us, axe in hand, cutting right and left, not the enemy, but the trees!

On Thursday evening we (Co. G) were ordered out to our picket post. We went out and took our "posish," expecting before morning to have a fight with the advance guard of the enemy. Long before midnight the fight commenced. It was bloody battle and lasted until sunrise. Company G fought silently but bravely, "nor lost a single man." That long night will ever be remembered by us and will remind us of our great battle with mosquitoes and gnats! ...

     Truly yours,   D.H.W. [7]

The clash with the rebels that the 7th Regiment had been eagerly seeking eventually came. After so many "cries of wolf" and the continual retreating of the Seventh's foe, Gen. John B. Floyd of the Confederate army advanced from Lewisburg and surprised Col. Tyler's soldiers at Cross Lanes. The results were not what the men in the 7th Ohio had dreamed and anticipated. The glowing romantic image of war and soldiering was seriously tarnished. The battle cost the regiment approximately 200 men.

The editor of the *Democrat* noted that the following letter had no date, but was written on the 23rd or 24th of August.

> Camp at Mouth of 20 Mile Creek, Va.
> 5 miles from Gauley Bridge.
> We went into camp at Cross Lanes, 9 miles from Summerville, on the 15th inst. (Aug.) and during that time the camp was in a continual state of excitement produced by the rumors of the enemy being in a large force and evidently coming down to wipe us out. They were estimated at from 10,000 to 20,000 and coming in two divisions – one to attack Gen. Cox at Gauley and the other to attack the Ohio 7th, whose orders were to hold all the ferries and fords of the Gauley River near Cross Lanes, and if attacked to fall back contesting the road inch by inch. We had guards at the Fords and Ferries and destroyed a number of boats to keep the rebels from getting across and attacking us in the rear. Our "Snake Hunters," scouts, returned every day with mere rumors received from people on the road but did not succeed in finding any of their pickets or advance guard until the 20th. Lieut. Nitscheim of Co. K, when out with a scouting party, captured a Rev. Capt. Sparr of the Rebel Home Guards, and he, under threats, told that he saw Floyd pass through Lewisburg with 900 men and 9 pieces of artillery coming in our direction, and that a heavy force under Wise was at White Sulphur Springs and were to march on Cox by way of Charleston – but having heard of the enemy so often before with- out being able to find them, did not place much reliance in the report, but still kept out strong pickets in all directions. At about 5 o'clock P.M. a messenger arrived saying that one of our pickets had been shot at and wounded by the rebel pickets. The Colonel rode out to the Ferry to see about matters and when he returned a dispatch awaited him at his quarters from Gen. Cox ordering him forward at once in this direction. While he was reading the dis- patch, a "Snake Hunter" arrived, saying that Capt. Shutte [Schutte] of Co. K was mortally wounded, 6 or 7 men also wounded and in the hands of the rebels, they having run into an encampment while scouting across the river on the Saturday Road …
> They report having killed a number of the enemy's cavalry,

men, and horses but cannot tell how many as they had to retreat to save themselves.

While writing, one of the prisoners has just arrived, having made his escape and bringing away two guns of the enemy, but being hotly pursued, had to drop them in the river as he was swimming across – the enemy's bullets whistling around his head without injuring him.

Our Colonel is now at Gauley Bridge to see Gen. Cox, and I presume we will get further orders on his return, but to what point cannot give a guess, but will let you know some time soon if we can get near mail communication ...

Yours truly, T.B. [8]

[T. B. is most likely Frederick T. Brown, the Chaplain of the 7th Regiment. Brown resigned on Nov. 15, 1861, and there is no more correspondence from T. B. after this letter. However, there was a Sgt. Thomas C. Brown in Co. B, who was killed at Cedar Mountain on August 8, 1862.]

Camp Near Gauley,
Thursday, August 22nd, 1861.
Eds. Democrat:

We left Somerville the 15th, going Westwardly about eight miles and taking an advantageous position at a place called Cross Lanes, where the leading Turnpike from the South crosses the Turnpike leading to Gauley, and about four miles from the Ferry on the Gauley river. The Snake Hunters with Company K took possession of the Ferry and also of the ford some seven miles down – Strong picket guards were stationed out in order to prevent all possibility of a surprise. We took several prisoners, among them a Captain, an old man of fifty years, I should think at least. But the rebels were equally alert, wounding several of our scouts, and wounding Captain Shontz [Schutte] of Company K and fourteen of his men and taking them prisoners. This affair happened on the 20th. They also took several of the Snakes but they all escaped. On the evening of the 20th, orders were received from Gen. Cox stationed at Gauley to march in immediately to join him. It was a beautiful evening, it being so light that Company F [the Franklin Rifles] had been out drilling by moonlight and had just come in and laid down for the night. We were immediately routed out, and in half an hour everything was packed and ready for the march. We started at 11 P.M. and marched steadily with an occasional halt for breathing until 11 A.M. when we camped, being as near to Gauley as we can get, and have a good camping ground. Each man carried his gun and cartridge box with thirty to forty rounds, also a knapsack, haversack, and canteen. The men endured the march well, but very few falling out. We are camped directly on the banks of the Gauley river, Gauley Bridge being situated at the mouth of the river at its junction with the Kanawha. You have probably heard of the capture of Captain Sprague of Company E, which with the late loss of Captain Shoutz makes four commandants of Companies that are absent. Capt. Seymour of Company G and Capt. Clayton of Company F being sick. Lieutenant Kimball of Company A now commands Company F. It is rumored this morning that the 11th Ohio Regiment stationed about five miles distant keep up a continual skirmish warfare with the rebels. It appears that Gov. Wise (or "G. Wise," as we call him) has been strongly reenforced, and together with his young hopeful O. Jennings, is determined to recover the ground he has lost and re- establish his military renown among the F.F.V's. There is a probability now of something of a battle before long. The advancing column from Clarksburg is strongly fortified at Sutton and Gen. Cox's Division is concentrating at Gauley Bridge.

      The health of the regiment is as good as usual. The surgeon reporting but ten under hospital care.

Everett [9]

[F.F.V. stands for First Families of Virginia. Thus, an F.F.V. was a member or descendant of such a family. Here, the term is probably used in a sarcastic manner. At his time in 1861, some Maryland troops referred to them as Fast Footed Virginians since they showed a willingness to run. [10]]

      In the aftermath of the battle of Cross Lanes, Everett summed up the physical condition and attitude of the 7th Ohio. His letter written ten days later shows the resiliency of youth and the fact that the war was going to continue for his regiment. Nevertheless, the boys appear to be tired and depressed after their first major encounter with the rebels.

In a fight where so many men were killed, wounded, and taken prisoners there was certainly to be close scrutiny of the actions of the commanding officer. In this respect Col. Tyler received a positive endorsement on the front page of the hometown newspaper. Then there was the sad and difficult task of notifying the relatives of those who had died. A compassionate letter from Col. Tyler to the widow of Capt. John Dyer exhibits the deep sorrow of the event, the Captain's bravery, and the fine character of Col. Tyler.

The newspapers may have lionized Col. Tyler, but his superior officers were not as kind in their official reports concerning the fight at Cross Lanes. [11]

Gen. Cox to Gen. Rosecrans – August 27, 1861.

"The Seventh keep straggling in. I do not think the number of killed large from all I can learn, but a good many are prisoners or scattered. Less than half are now here. All their train is safe here. Colonel Tyler will give me an official report to-day ... The force opposed to the Seventh is said by a prisoner to have been in that neighborhood some time, but was joined by a part of that up New River. They have made no new attack. The prisoner stated the number near Summersville at 3,000, with three pieces of cannon, and says a similar force is still up the New River and has been attacking our advance there. Our men are alert and confident, and all duty required is cheerfully done."

Gen. Cox to Gen. Rosecrans – Second message of the 27th.

"... Colonel Tyler was encamped at the cross-roads called Cross-Lanes, a part of his force on each road. The enemy were between him and Carnifix Ferry, about two miles from him. While his men were at breakfast in the morning they outflanked him and commenced the attack on both flanks and front nearly simultaneously. The regiment did not get in good shape for defense at any time, and was soon broken up and scattered."

George L. Hartsuff, Asst. Adj.-Gen., to Gen. Cox – August 27, 1861.

"Your dispatch of the 27th received. The commanding general is gratified with its definiteness. He regrets to say that the report concerning the seventh furnishes another evidence of the great deficiency, not to say inefficiency and worthlessness, of the performances of picket guard duty. From what appears it is plain that no adequate picket guards were posted by Colonel Tyler, or that his position was chosen without precaution. The duty with which he was charged required him to keep his regiment posted in mass in a position where his retreat could not be cut off, with strong picket guards and advanced pickets thrown well to the front to give timely notice of the enemy's approach and check any movement except in force. The commanding general hopes that this most unfortunate lesson will not be lost on the rest of his command. While he takes pleasure in saying your reports indicate better precautions, he hopes you will take occasion to deepen the lesson we have learned at such cost."

Gen. Cox to Gen. Rosecrans – August 28, 1861.

"The chaplain and surgeon of [the] Seventh are returned. They were not permitted to see the wounded. The enemy's officers treated them well. Reported 15 of ours killed and about 50 wounded. One captain killed and 1 a prisoner. About 300 are yet in the hills. The note refusing to let them see the wounded was signed by Floyd, and was courteous in language, assuring them that the wounded were sent over Gauley and were well taken care of. They were not allowed to go far enough within lines to judge the force, cavalry pickets being some miles this side of Cross-lanes. Our pickets on the Fayette road were fired into by a party of mounted men early this morning; 1 killed, 2 wounded. No further news up New River. A party has gone in advance to see what can be learned. They generally keep their infantry out of reach, attacking our outposts and scouting parties with cavalry ..."

Gen. Cox to Gen. Rosecrans – August 27th, 9 P.M.

"Major Casemate has carried over 400 of the Seventh into Charleston handsomely. He went by Big Sandy and down Elk. There are so many practicable routes for cavalry and infantry without trains that his presence in Charleston may prove very fortunate ..."

Gen. McClellan to Gen. Rosecrans – August 29, 1861.

"There is no excuse for Tyler being surprised. Concentrate everything possible against Floyd ..."

Gauley Bridge, Va., Sept. 11, 1861.
Ed. Democrat:

Since the battle at Cross Lane the 7th regiment has lain by, pretty much used up. Company F and what remains of Companies A, E, K, and O still remain at Gauley. The remaining Companies are at Charleston under Major Casemate. In spite of my precautions I gave you rather an exaggerated report in my former letter. Capt. Sterling of Company I, who was reported killed, has turned up all right at Charleston. Also, Capt. Asper, who was reported wounded and a prisoner, is now at Charleston safe and sound. Lieut. Wilcox of Company E, however, is a prisoner. Also Lieut. Cross of Company C was wounded and captured. As I stated before our whole loss amounts to nearly two hundred, but the men have undergone so much exposure that it is beginning to tell on them. There are but few who are dangerously sick and also but few who are really well. (I speak of those at Gauley.) Nearly all have some disposition however, that renders them unfit for duty –

Since entering Virginia, we have been essentially a scouting regiment, and as a matter of course, have been almost continually on the move, often making forced marches and working at all hours both night and day. It is no wonder then that the men begin to give out and become unfit for duty. We are lying here now awaiting orders from headquarters. A correct representation of the state of the regiment has been made to gen. Rosecrans, and I presume to say that we will be allowed to rest and recruit up before being ordered into the service. The men all hope that they will not be ordered into Virginia again, if they once get out of it, declaring the country "not worth fighting for."

The country is evidently wealthy in mineral wealth but requires the energy of free labor to bring it forth. I have seen as yet but three or four extensive plantations, but everywhere the blighting influence of slavery is visible. Weston may have contained one thousand inhabitants, Glenville about three hundred, Summerville possibly two hundred; Gauley Bridge contains two taverns, two stores, and three or four dwelling houses. The extensive bridge at this place which cost Virginia $30,000 was burnt down by Wise when he retreated.

A continued skirmish had been going on with the rebels, but they evidently consider us too well fortified to approach very near.

EVERETT [12]

Gauley Bridge, Va.
Saturday, Sept. 21, 1861.

Ed. Democrat:
You will perceive by the heading of this letter that we still remain in Gauley; and from the present appearances we are likely to do so for a considerable length of time.

Gen. Cox left here to advance up the New River towards Lewisburg on the 12th. Gen. Rosecrans had previously driven Floyd out of Cross lane and he (Floyd) had retired and formed a junction with Wise, and they together had encamped about fifteen miles from Gauley on the Richmond and Kanawha turnpike. The General gave out the order to march on the night of the 11th. Accordingly, on the 12th reveille was sounded at 3 A.M. The whole encampment soon presented a lively scene – men rushing around drawing and cooking the rations. Three days rations were drawn and cooked; knapsacks packed, guns cleaned, and the able-bodied men ready to leave by 5 A.M., leaving the sick and weak behind in charge of the tents.

We were ferried across the Gauley and then marched off as fast as we could and allow the flanking parties to work. We had not proceeded far beyond our lines before old "secesh' camp grounds began to make their appearance. We could easily tell, when quite a distance off, of our approach to one by the disagreeable odor. In many places the fences were lined with beef hides, and occasion- ally a dead horse lying at the road side added much to the purity of the atmosphere, especially as the weather was very hot and the roads quite dusty.

At a place called Hawks Nest, about eight miles from Gauley, the rebels had thrown up fortifications of some little importance, but we found them deserted. Still further on we found evidence of their packing up and leaving on short notice. The smoke was still rising from their camp fires, and fresh cavalry tracks were plainly visible. They had no tents and their "bush shanties" looked fresh as if recently made. It was intended that Gen. Rosecrans should advance a column from Cross Lane and cut off the retreat of the rebels to Lewisburg, while Gen. Cox advanced from Gauley, thus compelling the rebels to fight at a disadvantage or to make an unconditional surrender. But for some reason the column from Rosecrans failed to come up in time. Accordingly, after pursuing them until it was evident that they had made their retreat good to Lewisburg, the column was halted and the men bivouacked for the night. The 7th being in the rear, occupied a portion of the main camping ground of Floyd's and Wise's forces. It was on the land and near the residence of a Union man by the name of

Wood, who with his son were in Richmond, prisoners. They had completely destroyed and demolished everything except the bare walls.

In a very extensive orchard near the house not an apple was to be found. From the old documents, wills, deeds, etc., found in and around the house, it appears that the owner (Wood) was a man of great importance. Corporal Gridley of Company F found a deed or grant of fifteen hundred acres of land signed by "P. Henry, Esq., Governor of the Commonwealth of Virginia." He also found his (Wood's) commission of Major in the State Militia dated, I think, 1828. Also letters from Jonathan Edwards. Others found documents signed by H. Clay, all of which were carefully preserved, the men manifesting a great anxiety to get possession of them. We remained encamped there until the afternoon of the 15th.

In the morning, Col. Tyler, accompanied by Capt. Crane of Company A, started to see Gen. Rosecrans, who with the 23rd regiment remained at Cross Lanes [Gauley]. They got into Gauley on the morning of the 16th. It is said that the General complimented our Colonel very highly for his management at Cross Lane, only wondering "How any of us got away." He also gave him the command of the Kanawha Valley, while Gen. Cox with him advanced on toward Lewisburg. [Gen. Rosecrans' attitude toward Col. Tyler obviously mellowed since his correspondence of August 27th.]

We left our camp a little before four P.M. and reached Gauley before eight, marching the eighteen miles in four hours. A Sergeant of Company E who was wounded and taken prisoner at Cross lane had his arm amputated below the elbow and was left behind in the retreat. He says that the rebels have two thousand sick between here and Richmond on account of exposure.

Lieut. Cross of Company C was left behind at Cross Lane and has come into camp. He looks very bad. The ball struck his arm above the elbow, and glancing upward, lodged in the shoulder. It is to be feared that he will lose his arm. Private McCain of Company A was buried last night with the honors of war.

More soon.   EVERETT [13]

COL. E. B. TYLER – 7th REGIMENT
"W.D.B.," the correspondent of the Cincinnati Commercial,

writing from Camp Scott on Cross lanes Battle Ground, Va., under date of Sept. 17th, says:

"Col. Tyler visited the General yesterday. I am pleased to say that the General is satisfied with his conduct in the battle of Cross Lanes. His own statements concerning that affair have been generally substantiated by other testimony. It is true that he made a manly fight, and that if he had been supported by 500 more men, he would have thrashed Floyd's whole force. Tyler's men say that he exposed his own person most gallantly, and that he could have retreated successfully with his regiment without fighting if he had desired to do so. It is also true that he captured a rebel flag in the fight. His own regimental flag was preserved by a sturdy German. Colonel Tyler ordered him to cut off the flag staff, roll up the flag, and bring it to him. "By Jing," said the Dutchman, "dey no gets it. I fetches him to you." Three days afterwards the honest fellow delivered the precious flag to his Colonel at Gauley Bridge. Our total loss at that affair was 15 killed, about 40 wounded, and according to rebel statements, about 120 prisoners." [14]

From the Painesville (O.) Press and Advertiser

Gauley, Va., Sept. 1861.

Mrs. John N. Dyer, Painesville, O.

My Dear Madam: Permit me to introduce myself to you in this hour of your terrible trial and affliction, as a friend of him who now, within the lines of the enemy's camp, "Sleeps the sleep that knows no waking;" as a friend to him who must have been to you what all else on earth cannot replace. Allow me to intrude upon you, and for a moment mingle my sorrow with your tears for one we loved and esteemed.

While you, madam, and those little ones around you mourn the loss of a beloved husband and father, our Regiment joins with you in your sorrow for the loss of one of our country's bravest and truest defenders, and we an esteemed friend and officer, whose counsels and assistance we have appreciated.

I saw him fall while leading on his brave men in obedience to my orders. His last words were, when I asked him if he could turn the enemy's advancing column and prevent them from out-flanking us, "I will try sir. Company, forward, by file left, march!" His order to fire soon followed; a moment after he was struck by a musket ball and Capt. Dyer's earthly career was closed. Yet while we deeply mourn his death, it is some satisfaction to know the enemy paid dearly for his loss. – Their disordered ranks and halting column showed clearly that his efforts were successful, although it cost his life and that of some of his men. No officer of the line commanded more universal respect, had more of my confidence than did Capt. Dyer, and we mourn his loss as deeply as can any one, save you, and the little flock made fatherless by his sudden death.

My prayer is that He who holds the destinies of the Universe in His hand may be your protector and a father to your orphan children. If I can serve you in any way, you have only to command me. Very respectfully your obedient Servant,

E. B. TYLER
Col. 7th O.V., U.S.A. [15]

Operations for the 7th Ohio now centered at Charleston and Gauley Bridge. Between the mountainous terrain and the inclement weather, it was not a pleasant sojourn.

LETTER FROM THE ARMY

Extract from a letter dated Gauley Bridge, Sept., written by R. W. Orvis to his parents in Ravenna: [Eighteen year old Recellus Orvis was a private in Co. G. On Nov. 1, 1863 he was appointed Principal Musician.]

"You will see by this that we have left Charleston. We are at present enjoying the hospitality of the part of the regiment that was stationed at this place. There are only one hundred of us who came here from Charleston. It is called Company L, being made up of parts of Companies I, H, and G. We left Charleston a week ago yesterday to go, as they told us, on a three days' scout; but the first day we went on the boat only up to Camp Enyart, eleven miles up the river. Here we stayed till Tuesday morning, sleeping on the ground both nights previous. Tuesday morning we prepared for a march. We here got our overcoats, which are just the thing for these cold nights. We shall draw our winter blankets soon. Some have drawn them already, and they are a nice thing. After leaving Camp Enyart, we marched 12 ½ miles and halted for the night and went to bed in a pile of straw. In the morning we went nine miles further, when we halted till two o'clock. We then crossed the Kanawha river and got three days rations preparatory to going on a scout. We stayed here till two o'clock Thursday when we were re-enforced by four Kentucky Companies under Major Leper. We then all started off together up "Luke creek." We crossed this creek forty-eight times, getting our feet wet nearly every time. It commenced raining and we took up our quarters under some lumber piles and in a sawmill; but I did not sleep much, my clothes were so wet. In the morning, we found it had been raining all night, and the creek had so swollen that we had to take another road. We started off, it raining all the time. Our road lay along the bed of a small stream. We marched almost all day in water up to our knees and sometimes deeper, when in the afternoon we came to Laurel creek which we could not cross. We felled several large trees but it was of no use, the current carrying them away; so we encamped for the night. I slept (or tried to sleep) in a small cabinet shop with a few others of our Company. In the morning we found that the stream had fallen so we could cross, but our provisions were given out. So the Major thought best to abandon the course we were going and take the nearest to camp. We accordingly started, but on arriving at the Ferry at the camp of this place, we found it had been washed away, and the river was so high and full of drift wood that we could not cross. But luckily for Company L we had left a barrel of crackers on the same side of the river when we started on the scout, and we went to them one and a half miles down river. – We had to climb along the side of the mountain for the road was overflowed. We found the provisions all right, and I believe that victuals never tasted better than that hard bread and raw pork. Luckily for us a steam boat had taken advantage of the high water and come up here with clothing for the army, and she took us across. We slept on the boat all night and came here yesterday morning."

(It was hardships and exposure like the foregoing, which Lieut. Robinson endured during his last scout, and which no doubt caused his death. – Ed. Democrat.) [Author's note: In the October 16 edition of the *Democrat* a column and a half was devoted to Lt. W. Henry Robinson of Company G, the Tyler Guards, who had died of "illness." In the next week's edition, there was nearly a full column on the death of Pvt. A. R. Butler, also of Company G. Pvt. Butler died from typhoid fever on October 10, 1861. [16]]

Charleston, Va., Nov. 10 [1861]
Ed. Democrat:
News? Well, there isn't any. Since the completion of our telegraph, trying to send news by letter is small business. And a few of us are conscious that there is any great world existing outside the narrow rim of these Kanawha hills. Speaking of hills reminds me of what one of our lank Virginia soldiers was heard to "get off" the other day. A few of them were returning from a long scout. In the rear was a cadaverous chap who wore an elderly looking hat, from the crown of which a few straight hairs stuck gracefully out. He had not spoken a word for the last five miles, when he suddenly "broke out" in this profane way: I k'n tell you how it cum to be so rough here: you see when the Lord got through makin' the world, he had about ten thousand hills left he didn't know what to do with – so he jes tumbled 'em all into Western Virginia."

There has been an uncomfortable suspense among the citizens of this place for a couple of weeks past, which is at last relieved by another flight of the old thief. The 7th was on hand at Gauley, and in following the rebels about thirty-two miles per- formed some more of the hard marching for which it is famous in this country. The greatest chagrin and indignation was felt among the men that Floyd and his army were not captured. Every intelligent body expected it. None but generals can see why it was not done. It does seem as if it might have been. Floyd and his army going into winter quarters at Columbus [in Ohio as prisoners] would have been a good accompaniment to our successes in Kentucky and on the coast and would have looked like business.

I might give you a page or two of "reliable information" as to where the 7th is going to winter, what is to be done in the Kanawha country, etc., but I think I had better save the trouble by simply stating that I don't know anything about it. The paymaster is expected here to-day; the 7th has not yet received "a red" since entering the service. The hospitals here contain some four or five hundred sick men.

It don't seem to me much like November, the season having been a mild one. Yet the woods are bare and hushed; no birds, no crickets are heard; a little ice has been formed; in the mornings and evenings long blue overcoats and noses abound, and "Autumn, like a faint old man sits down by the way-side aweary."

The guns with which our battery is furnished are Parrot's steel rifled ten pounders – rather heavy to handle, but bully to shoot.

I suppose the division of the old commonwealth at this time is thought by many at the North to be bad policy. It may be so, but let this contest result as it may, this part of the State must before long be free. [A reference to the formation of the State of West Virginia] There are few sections in the United States that offer greater inducements to Northern enterprise than this – to all which the Yankees are not blind. Through the folly of the F.F.V.'s their influence is fast departing and passing into the hands of Union men. The jealousy and hatred of Northern settlers can never again retard the development of the free element here as heretofore been done. This portion has long been unduly taxed in many ways to support Eastern Virginia, receiving in return contempt and neglect. Whether the division is politic or not, it is entirely natural. The producers and businessmen here – who constitute the real worth of the community – have everything to alienate them from and nothing to bind them to their distinguished nigger breeders across the mountains. Besides the thirty-nine counties now ready to form the State of Kanawha, there are several more who are anxious to do so as soon as they can be relieved of a little of the present rebel pressure. A strong effort will be made to make Charleston the new capital.

C. H. [17]

[C. H. is most likely 22 year old Charles Hummel of Co. F. He was mustered in as a private, and he was promoted to sergeant on August 27, 1862.]

Letter From Dr. I. Selby King.

Mrs. M. B. Skinner, President of the Ravenna Soldiers' Aid Society, has received the following letter from Dr. King, acknowledging the boxes sent from this Aid Society to the 7th Regiment.

Camp 7th regiment, O.V.U.S.A.,
Charleston, Va. 24th Nov., 1861.
Mrs. M. B. Skinner – Dear Madam:

The boxes from the Ravenna Aid Society, directed to my care arrived at this post on Thursday last week, in safety and in good order, and the contents were very acceptable to all concerned.

I shall think it necessary in future to specify what we want; it will be only necessary to say we want articles for the Hospital, and leave it to your judgment what to send.

The boxes contained the best assortment of articles for hospital use of any I have had the pleasure to inspect.

Please present to your Society the thanks of all the men in the 7th Regiment Hospital, for the many articles of comfort, and the many tokens of friendship the boxes contained. The distribution of letters, papers, and other tokens of kindness, awakened many pleasant thoughts and sweet memories of friends at home.

The sick of Co.'s F and G are all improving, and in fact all the patients at this post are on the gain. Only about one hundred of the 7th Regiment are in hospital now.

Accept my individual thanks and the thanks of all who are benefited by your donations.

Yours truly,
I. S. King, M.D. [18]

D.H.W.'s humor and writing style became a welcome sight for the *Democrat*'s editor and readers. The following letter was printed in the December 18 edition. Assuming the "24" is correct and judging by the content, the letter was written in November.

Charleston, Virginia
Dec. [Nov.] 24, 1861.
Editor Democrat –

The Seventh Ohio Regiment has again been surprised and surrounded! Not as at Cross Lanes by the traitor Floyd, but by a *sea of mud*! We have seen mud before, but never to such a depth nor of the same quality. It varies in depth from six to eighteen inches and is of the blackest and most adhesive kind.

Thursday last was observed as a day of Thanksgiving by the officers and men of the Seventh regiment, not however, as with the good citizens of Ohio, by good sermons, better suppers, and a good social time in general, but – the Paymaster had arrived with his iron chest, which was filled with glittering coin and those famous Treasury Notes. Joy beamed in every countenance and we all were thankful.

In the case of Camp Warren, "distance lends enchantment to the view." When viewed from the pilot house of a steamer, as she winds her way up or down the Kanawha, or from an adjoining hill, this camp with its straight rows of apparently white tents presents an appearance of neatness and comfort; but walk in and take a seat while we go away a half-mile or more, steal a rail, lug it to the foot of our alley, chop it, build a fire in the mud, slip through the mud down to the river with a large army kettle, fill it with water and climb up the bank somehow, place it over the fire, cut from off the "Idol of Cincinnati" a few slices, fry them, pour a pint of ground coffee into the "boiling Cauldron," and after a few minutes devoted to setting out a plate of *hickory chips!* And the *china dishes!* Present you and my comrades with a *bona fide*, genuine every day repast.

After partaking of our sumptuous fare, we enter the wigwam, for mind you the table stands outside, gather around the stove which is one size larger than a camp kettle, and while away the hours in numerous ways. Reading matter is rather scarce. The Cincinnati papers occasionally find their way to us, but rarely does a Portage County paper appear in camp. The boys in the Seventh are rapidly obtaining furloughs and visiting their "loved ones at home." Troops from Gauley and vicinity are almost daily moving down the river – Gen. Rosecrans passed through here on Monday on his way to Wheeling. Gen. Cox is expected here to-day. "Secesh" faces are as long as the moral law, and Federal Union faces are *visa versa!* In this once rebel hot-bed.

Respectfully,   D.H.W. [19]

Capt. Seymour was one of the fortunate ones to return to Ravenna. The *Portage County Democrat* reported the following.

Capt. F. A. Seymour arrived in Ravenna on Monday [Dec. 2] from the camp of the 7th Regiment. He brought no news of importance not already possessed by the public. It was not decided whether the 7th passes the Winter in Virginia or not. Capt, Seymour returns early next week and all letters left at the Ravenna Book Store this week will be taken by him to Camp Warren.

Capt. Seymour brought home a large number of letters from the Portage County boys. Dr. Willis had arrived and was installed as "Q.M." Chauncey Hickox and Chas. Gillis of Ravenna, who had been very sick, were out again. – The boys of Co. G were all in good spirits, and "good" for twice their number of "seceshers." The weather was milder than it is here, and the Regiment well equipped for Winter service.[20]

At this point in the war the involvement of Portage County was proudly stated in this item from the December 4th newspaper.

PORTAGE COUNTY has nobly done her duty – aye, more than her duty – in supplying men for the "O.V.U.S.A." Her quota is 653, and already seven hundred and sixty men are enrolled from among her brave sons. We have two companies in the 7th Regiment, two companies in the 42d, and one in the 41st; a six gun battery of Artillery – Capt. Cotter – a two gun battery of Artillery – Capt. King – and have furnished Colonels – Col. James A. Garfield, Col. Wm. B. Hazen, Col. E. B. Tyler. In the 2d Ohio Cavalry is nearly a company of Portage County boys – and in the 6th Cavalry O.V. there will be a full company. Major Stedman, of the 6th Cavalry, and Quartermaster Willis, of the 7th infantry, are from Portage County. These are the prominent items of our contribution in aid of the Government, and other details could be collected which would add much interest to this record, which we have not time to elaborate today. It will be conceded, we are sure, that scarce any County, in proportion to population and none has more cheerfully responded to the call of a bleeding country, than our own gallant Portage. [21]

Chapter Two

"something to be a soldier in winter"

Some members of the 7th Ohio Regiment were granted their wish; they were headed for a change of scenery. However, they were not going to hole up in snug winter quarters, nor receive a cushy furlough home. Part of their task was to keep open the route of the Baltimore and Ohio Railroad, which was a lifeline between the eastern theater of war and the mid-west states. It loomed as a battle with the winter elements as well as with the rebels.

   Romney, Hampshire Co., Va.,
   Thursday, Dec. 19, 1861.
Ed. Democrat:
  Could you this morning visit Romney, you would behold a splendid scene. On almost every eminence is seen the busy camp of some regiment, their many white tents covered with a heavy frost, glistening in the rays of the glorious sun. The clear waters of the Potomac flow gently past our camp on their winding way to old Ocean, and the Alleghenies rear their frowning heights in the distance.
  We, the Seventh Ohio Regiment, left Charleston on the Kanawha on Tuesday, the 11th, on board the steamers Fort Wayne and Stephen Decatur, and after a pleasant jaunt by river and railroad, arrived at Green Springs Thursday evening last. There we remained until Tuesday morning of this week, when we buckled on our knapsacks and started on foot for this place. The weather was fine and the roads in good condition, but the knapsacks being heavily loaded with clothing and blankets greatly worried the troops, and when we arrived here at six o'clock in the evening, we were a tired set of "bould sogers."
  Our tents are the new Sibley Patent and are a large, tall, and well ventilated kind. We are encamped upon a beautiful, dry hill west of the Court House, at the foot of which runs the South Branch of the Potomac. There are probably eight thousand troops now here, with

twenty pieces of cannon. The Ringold Cavalry from Pennsylvania and the Kelly Lancers from Western Virginia are also here. The Seventh Indiana Regiment arrived here last night, and two six gun batteries of artillery are expected here to day.

Every morning a large picket guard is sent out on the different roads leading into Romney, and a sharp lookout is kept as we daily expect an attack from the rebels. Skirmishing between our pickets and the rebel pickets is almost a daily occurrence upon the Winchester road, ours driving the enemy's every time. Hoping in my next to give you a description of a successful battle in this vicinity. I remain,

Yours respectfully,   D.H.W. [1]

FROM THE 7TH REGIMENT – THE VICTORY AT BLUE GAP

Camp Keys,
Romney, January 8th. [1862]

Eds. Herald: On Sunday last we received orders to draw four days rations and prepare for a march. All night, or nearly so, we were giving out clothing, drawing and cooking rations. All Monday we waited expecting orders. In the afternoon six companies were ordered out to be ready to march at one that night. Company B was selected as one of the six, and in a driving wind storm we started. Where we were going to no one knew, but imagined to Blue Gap, distant seventeen miles. [Blue Gap and Hanging Rock were the same location. [2]] What a tramp we had! You know how difficult it is to walk in sand, hard enough when it is pleasant weather, but doubly so when the snow is falling and the wind driving it in every direction. Nevertheless, orders are orders and must be obeyed.

The first part of the way we walked fast enough to keep warm, but after we had passed our pickets, we threw out flankers which kept us halting or marching very slowly, consequently, we suffered from the cold. About daybreak we came in sight of the Gap and were drawn up in line of battle. Our force was about 3,000 men, detachments from the 4th, 5th, 7th, and 8th Ohio, 14th Indiana, 1st Virginia, together with cavalry and a battery of six guns.

For the first time we succeeded in giving the rebels a surprise and returned the complement served us at Cross Lanes, by taking their breakfast away from them. The 4th and 5th were ordered out as flankers, the 8th in advance through the Gap. We came up to the

mouth of the Gap at a double quick, passed the cavalry who cheered us on. A smart fire was carried on for a few moments, when our *brave foe* took to their heels. When they came to their entrenchments, they found them filled with *live Yankees*, and suddenly came to the conclusion that –
"He who fights and runs away,
May live to fight another day."
The cavalry were ordered to the front for pursuit, the rout was complete and we of the 7th had the pleasure of seeing how we looked at Cross Lanes. Not a man was hurt on our side, several on the other side will never hold a gun again. So perish all rebels to such a Government. Our boys were very much disappointed that they did not have a chance. We captured all their tents, two cannon, a large amount of ammunition, burnt their houses, mills, and left the place a smoking ruins, and started for home reaching Romney at 4 P.M. having marched over 34 miles in a driving snow storm, fought a battle, routed the enemy over 1,800 strong in about 16 hours. That, I think, was accomplishing considerable in a very short time.

Soldiering in summer will pass, but excuse me from a winter campaign if it can be avoided. But what can't be cured must be endured. We were under the command of Major Casement, Lieut. Colonel Creighton having been injured by a fall from his horse, and Col. Tyler not having yet returned.

Yours,   J. T. S.[3]

[J. T. S. was 26 year old Capt. James T. Sterling of Co. B. On Sept. 1, 1862, he was promoted to Lt. Col. of the 103rd Ohio Volunteer Infantry.]

In early January, Gen. Stonewall Jackson's Confederates left Winchester, Virginia and moved into the area of Romney. It was Jackson's intent to tear up much of the railroad track of the Baltimore and Ohio and to destroy the dams along the Chesapeake and Ohio Canal. After the fight at Blue Gap, the Union forces decided to retreat. Capt. Sterling and a soldier calling himself "Cornelius" wrote letters regarding the withdrawal from Romney. A newspaper article in the *Democrat* exhibited discontent regarding the retreat of the Union troops.

Patterson's Creek, Jan. 12. [1862]

Eds. Herald: -- I wrote you on the 8th but now drop a line to let you know our whereabouts. We have had the hardest march the last day and night that we have as yet experienced. It is something to be a soldier in winter, but

"In God is our trust,
For our cause is just."

and if we suffer a little for our country, we are not worthy of such a country.

In my last I gave you an account of our expedition to Blue Gap and the result. After two days rest, we were ordered to hold ourselves in readiness to march at a moment's notice. At 7 in the evening we started, moved as far as the road and there in a driving winter rain had to wait until half past eleven before we could move on. Between the thaw and the rain the roads were shoe deep in mud, the streams all swollen – of which we had many to cross. We marched on until about three in the morning when we were ordered to rest. I procured three rails and in about two minutes was fast asleep on them. About five we started again, and on we marched till seven at night – rain pouring down all the time – when we reached this place, which is on the Baltimore and Ohio R. R., which contains one house.

Why we have made that retreat, none of us can tell, except it was rumored that 20,000 men were marching on Romney. We are fortifying here and intend, I suppose, making a stand if the enemy advances. We are but eight miles from Cumberland, and I suppose the rebels desire to gain this place, as it is a town of some size. But they will have to fight for it. We have been obliged to send away our baggage, and I have nothing but what I have on my back. This paper I had to borrow.

Lieut. Eaton arrived this morning and is out on picket tonight.

Yours,   J. T. S. [4]

Patterson's Creek, Hampshire Co., Va.
January 15th, 1862.

At the time of our last writing our Camp was all astir in regard to the expedition to Ballou's [Blue] Gap. There were detachments from several Regiments engaged. The 4th, 5th, 6th, 7th, and 8th Ohio, 1st and 7th Virginia, 14th Indiana Infantry, in all nineteen hundred men. Parts of several companies of Cavalry, 300 men, with Downs six gun battery, two steel guns, and one mountain howitzer.

They left Romney at midnight, Monday, January 6th, and arrived at the Gap at 7 A.M. Tuesday.

The enemy were surprised completely and scattered like

sheep before the charge of the Cavalry. Fifteen were killed, twenty wounded, and several taken prisoners. Two pieces cannon, twelve horses, four wagons, beside small arms, camp equipage, etc., were captured. – The troops engaged arrived in camp at 7 P.M., after a march of thirty-two miles, made in sixteen hours.

Many of them were so exhausted as to hardly be able to reach camp. Col. Tyler arrived in camp Thursday last, where he was soon welcomed by nearly the whole Regiment, all eager to learn the news from home or at least catch a glimpse of a man who has seen home.

On Friday afternoon, orders were given to pack up, strike tents, and be ready to move at a moment's notice. Rumors were afloat that an attack was anticipated, but Jeff's followers appeared not; doubtless thinking 'discretion the better part of valor.'

After hasty preparation, we left our camp at 8 P.M. and marched to town, where we awaited the movement of other Regiments. Here we waited until 12 ½ A.M., when the column moved toward Springfield.

The 7th arrived at that place at 5 A.M. Fires were kindled and we bivouacked for the night, (or what was left of it.)

Some wrapped themselves in their blankets and threw them selves on the frosty ground while others more cautious in regard to health, placed rails between their bodies and the damp ground and slept soundly.

Next morning, after a hasty meal, the column again "fell in."

When noon came, six miles had been wearily passed and we bivouacked. After resting an hour on straw, "realized" from a Secesh straw stack, we marched on through mud, water, and a drenching rain until dark, when we pitched our "moving tents" in a great field of mud. Here we still remain and report "all quiet on the Potomac."

Yours truly,
Cornelius. [5]

WITHDRAWAL FROM ROMNEY – The retreat our forces were obliged to make from Romney was so sudden that "adequate transportation" could not be had, and about all that could not be carried by men, was burned. From a private letter from a member of the 7th, we [the editors of the *Portage County Democrat*] learn that the regiment lost much valuable camp equipage. Co. C – the Oberlin company – lost all their tents but one; Co. F lost two tents, Co. G one tent. – Other companies suffered similar losses. King's Battery lost three or five tents. Boxes, clothing, guns, spades, and cooking utensils were lost in considerable numbers. The 7th left Romney at 12 ½ o'clock at night, Friday, January 10, and on Saturday reached Patterson Creek Station, on the Balt. And O. R.R., where they now are. This point is twenty miles from Romney. At the time this letter was written – the 15th – it was some expected that the 7th would fall back eight miles farther to Cumberland.

Gen. Lander ordered the retreat to foil some supposed "trap" the rebels had set for his forces – but the movement looks as if quite needless. If it was necessary to evacuate Romney, it is not easy to understand why the rebel town was not burned, instead of leaving it to fall into the hands of the enemy, for *their* Winter quarters – when our men are marched away, and their tents burned. [6]

As the winter wore on, the 7th Ohio settled in at Patterson's Creek for a few weeks. With more free time in camp, there was an increase in soldier correspondence from a variety of writers to the newspapers. Of particular note was the promotion of Col. Tyler to the command of the Third Brigade and Lt. Col. William R. Creighton replacing Tyler in command of the 7th Ohio.

Patterson's Creek, Va.
January 18, 1862.

... Gen. Kelly has resigned his command of the forces here on account of ill health. Gen. Lander is his successor. The forces yesterday were divided into three brigades and will be commanded respectively by Col. Tyler of the Seventh Ohio, Col. Dunning of the 5th Ohio, and Col. Kimball of the Fourteenth Indiana. The regiments in Tyler's Brigade are the 7th Ohio, 7th Indiana, 1st Virginia,, and 10th Pennsylvania; also the Ringold Cavalry and Daum's Battery of Artillery. This will be a crack brigade.

Why Romney was evacuated by our forces I do not pretend to say, but presume it was for the best. The rebels have now possession of the town, but I do not think they will hold it long unless they work *like thunder* for it, as we intend going there to clean them out to day or to morrow.

Last night a reconnoitering party composed of Companies A and F of the Ohio Seventh and two companies each from the other regiments of Tyler's Brigade run down on a special train to Capin Bridge, 13 miles below here, to "see what we could see," and after scouting around for some time without getting sight of a Southern Confederacy and being convinced that if there had been any there they had "lit out" on our approach, we returned to camp about ten o'clock, "pulled the drapery of our couch about us and lay down to pleasant dreams," which however, were broken off at an early hour this morning by the sound of "the ear piercing fife and the soul stirring drum," and the stentorian voice of our Orderly calling out: "Company A, turn out for roll call!" It was then, as we drew on a pair of frozen boots covered with mud about an inch thick, that the interrogation might have escaped our lips, "Who wouldn't be a soldier?"

Orders have been issued to keep three days' rations cooked ready for a march, and present indications favor an advance on Romney soon – *very soon*. Tyler's Brigade is to lead the van and open the ball, and the others will move up and participate if neces- sary. It will not be many days before something "big" will come to pass on this portion of the "sacred sile." *"Onward to Romney!"* is the sentiment here.

Hoping in my next to be able to furnish something of more interest to you and your readers, and that it may be dated from Romney instead of this poor, miserable, God forsaken mud-hole, I remain as ever,

    Very respectfully, D. G. S.
              Co. A, 7th Reg. [7]

       Camp Kelly, Patterson's Creek, Va.,
         Wednesday, Jan. 29, 1862.
Editor Democrat:

"All is quiet on the Potomac" yet, but from what can be seen one would judge that before long this *quietness* will be "played out," at least in this, the Western Division of the grand army of the Potomac, which is under command of the brave and gallant General Lander. Long trains, heavily laden with Ohio's patriotic sons, almost daily arrive at this camp which is now swelled to a monster one. The 29th Ohio Regiment has been added to the Third Brigade and is a fine body of soldiers. The Third Brigade, under command of Col. Tyler, is now composed of the 1st Virginia, 7th Indiana, 29th Ohio, 110th Pennsylvania and 7th Ohio regiments, the Ringold Cavalry and Domb's [Daum's] Battery. A fine company of Sharpshooters from Boston, Massachusetts, having rifles weighing from forty to sixty pounds with telescope sights, and which will kill every time at a mile distant, are here. They are all a sure shot. These rifles are carried about in a neat wagon, and are calculated to be used in a long range. Col. Tyler is each day engaged in drilling his brigade, which he intends making the "crack brigade" of this division. Col. Tyler's Aids are Adjutant DeForest and Lieut. Quay. Company G is commanded by Lieut. S. S. Reed. Drum major Woodard arrived last evening. The Seventh Ohio will soon have a full Martial Band – twelve fifes and twelve drums. Our Silver Cornet Band members are spending a short furlough at home. Gen. Jackson, the rebel General, is still at Romney. Our sick are doing well at Cumberland. Mud is deep and – "all is quiet on the Potomac."

Respectfully,   D. H. W. [8]

Patterson's Creek, Jan. 30, 1862.

Ed. Democrat:

Even here in this benighted land, hemmed in as we are by mountains and rivers, occasionally we hear a word or two in regard to what is going on through the medium of the press. By the last mails we have learned of the success of the Portage county boys in Eastern Kentucky. It caused a thrill of exultation in our camp when we knew that Col. GARFIELD had met the enemy with such success. We feel that we are honored, for we too, are from old Portage. We do not envy their laurels, but I know it is the desire of every member of the 7th to emulate their energy. Prominent among the queries of the camp are these: "When shall we move on? When shall we advance?"

The great mass of the Northern soldiers entered upon this struggle, not for the novelty of it, not for the comfort, nor for the gain. They enlisted for the earnest intention of fighting. They expected to endure danger, fatigue, hunger, cold, and watchfulness.

They expected to strike down rebellion with desperate energy, for they felt that the danger demanded great sacrifices to avert it. They still look for hard work, and beyond this they look with patient waiting to the time when the work for which they engaged shall have been accomplished, and they may return to their homes. When this is done, and no sooner, will they return, rejoicing that our Government still exists, but sorrowing for the brave messmates who will not return ... [The rest of the letter contains a long list of officers' names and their positions.]

CORNELIUS [9]

On February 5, 1862 the activity for the 7th Ohio and the Third Brigade began to increase. They were on the move again. The exploits of their cavalry in a skirmish drew admirable responses from the infantry.

The Seventh Ohio rejoiced over Union victories elsewhere, especially the capture of Fort Donelson where their old nemesis from Cross Lanes, Gen. John B. Floyd, made his escape and left Gen. Simon Buckner to surrender the Confederate forces to Gen. Ulysses Grant.

The celebration of George Washington's Birthday in the mid-1800's was akin to the Fourth of July, and the soldiers of the 7th Ohio duly noted this important holiday.

Camp Sprague, Jersey Mountain, Va.
Wednesday, February 12th, 1862.

Here we are at the summit of Jersey Mountain, bivouaced in huts made of the limbs and brush of the many pine trees which crown this mountain. On Wednesday morning last, the Third Brigade under command of Col. Tyler were ordered to move, and shortly after, we were aboard the cars and moving slowly down the railroad leaving behind our tents, knapsacks, etc. in the care of the few who were soon to follow us. When a few miles below the South branch of the Potomac, we left the railroad and bivouaced in some pine woods until 9 o'clock in the evening, when we commenced moving slowly up the mountain road. The moon shone most brilliantly down upon the silent five thousand, who with nothing but blanket, well-filled haversack, cartridge box and gun, were cheerfully marching toward the foe. On reaching the valley of the Little Cappicon on the other side of Jersey Mountain, we halted and built fires using the fence rails for firewood. A grander or more sublime scene I never saw than these many brilliant fires surrounded by the seeming myriad of human life.

In a short time the column commenced moving forward. The Little Cappicon was now to be crossed, and there was no bridge on which to cross the foaming, surging, little river. Col. Tyler, his aide and the Ringold Cavalry were soon busied in taking us across until a temporary foot-bridge could be built. Again we marched on, and when within two miles of Frenchtown, which is on the pike running from Romney to Winchester, we halted, built fires, and lay down to rest, having learned that the rebels had left Romney.

At four o'clock on Thursday afternoon, greatly disappointed, we started back. Crossed the Little Cappicon and bivouaced for the night, using a large stack of unthreshed wheat for bedding. The next morning we came back up this mountain and have been here ever since, without tents or knapsacks. Saturday afternoon the 7th Regiment turned to greet Col. Sprague of the 63rd Ohio, formerly Captain of Company E of our Regiment. Col. Tyler is daily drilling the gallant Third Brigade. Gen. Lander says the "Third" is to be in front of his column. We are lying here for some good reason I have no doubt. Gen. Lander's *head is level.* We will doubtless move *somewhere* to-day. –

The "Democrat" is a welcome visitor in camp and is now regularly received. Snow is nearly six inches in depth on Jersey Mountain, and the winds blow cold and harsh through our pine huts. A fire of pine logs is burning before our hut, smoking us *beautifully!* Out time is merely passed in drilling, cleaning guns, carrying logs, making coffee, frying pork on a stick, cooking in our tin cups an entirely new dish called "Dope," telling yarns, writing letters, and singing. Hoping to date my next letter somewhere else, I remain respectfully, D. H. W. [10]

Camp Pawpaw,
Feb. 16, 1862.

Ed. Democrat:

The present writing finds the Third Brigade encamped at the above named place, situated about two miles South-East from Pawpaw Station on the Baltimore & Ohio Rail Road, and some eight miles North-West from Bloom's Furnace on the Winchester Pike. Leaving Camp Cross Roads on the morning of the 13th, we arrived here about six o'clock P.M. of the same day, where we now await "further orders." Gen. Landers, who preceded us from Pawpaw Station, moved on with three regiments of infantry and about 1,500 cavalry to Bloom's Furnace, where was reported some 800 rebel militia who were expecting Jackson with reinforcements. The cavalry reached the secesh camp at an early hour in the morning but found it totally depopulated. The rebels had "dug out" leaving their empty entrenchments, a few old wagons, and a few other "traps" behind. Pursuing them a short distance further, the cavalry discovered the devils on the top of a mountain in the bushes, ready for "bush whacking." The cavalry willing to try them at their own game, immediately dismounted and made a "break" for them, when the bushwhacking began in earnest and was kept up for some minutes when the rebels retired on the "double quick" principle, leaving twenty of their dead and about as many wounded, among whom was one Colonel, two Captains, and three Lieutenants. Our loss was two killed and one wounded – perhaps mortally.

The enemy's force engaged in the fight numbered 700. The infantry being some distance in the rear of the cavalry did not reach the scene of action in time to see the fun. It is said that the entire rebel force could have been captured had the First Virginia Cavalry obeyed orders. It seems they were ordered by Gen. Lander ahead to cut off the retreat, which they refused to do, saying that the road was lined with breastworks. I do not vouch for the truth of the above, but tell it only as it was told to me. Gen. Lander led our forces and was in the thickest of the "brush," – proving himself what he is already known to be – a cool, clear headed, and brave commander.

Capt. O'Brien, Gen. Landers' First Aid, was brought in this evening, wounded in the left shoulder. He, with a squad of the First Ohio Cavalry, went out reconnoitering about twelve miles South of here on the Winchester Pike, when riding up to a farm house they were accosted by the "proprietor" who told them that there was a saddle in the barn, and side arms, which he "reckoned" belonged to some of our men that had been killed near there a day or two previous. The Captain, suspecting nothing wrong, ordered some of the men to go and get the "traps." On reaching the barn, however, they found several saddles – all fitted too with secesh cavalry men – who at once opened fire upon them. Capt. O'Brien, hearing the report of the fire-arms, immediately repaired to the spot and meeting a rebel, he was asked, "Who are you?" I'm a Union man, G-d d-n you!" replied the Captain, at the same time drawing his holster and firing at the devil, but unfortunately missing his aim. The rebel fired about the same time, his shot passing through the left shoulder of Capt. O'Brien. By this time the skirmish had become pretty general. Capt. O'Brien, after he was wounded, led a charge against the enemy and himself succeeded in sending one of them to that bourne from which no "sojer" returns. But owing to the enemy's superiority in numbers, and Capt. O'Brien becoming faint from the wound he had received, our men were forced to retire. The rebels numbered about fifty cavalry, and some infantry, while our force numbered but twenty-five cavalry. Several of the rebels "shuffled off their mortal coil." None of our men were hurt except Capt. O'Brien and his wound is not considered dangerous, though it may disable him for some time.

How long we remain here I am unable to say, but hope not for long, as the boys are all anxious to move on Winchester, which will probably be our next march.

The news that reaches us almost daily of Union victories everywhere is very encouraging, and it is thought by many that a few more months' good fighting will wind up the war. I hope the prediction will prove correct and may God speed the day for our glorious flag to wave triumphantly over every rebel State, and for our noble bird to be permitted to spread its wings from ocean to ocean; and its tail drooping in the Gulf of Mexico, and its beak tipping the waters of Lake Superior unmolested for ages to come.

D. G. S.
Co. A, 7th Reg't. [11]

3d Brigade,
Camp Tyler, Va., February 17, 1862.
Ed. Democrat:

Since my last writing, events of great and momentous importance have transpired, and are, ere this, doubtless household words among you.

Mill Springs, Roanoke, Fort Henry, Donelson, and Savannah!

Are these not enough to make one's breast swell with pride – his eyes dilate with patriotic fire, as he reflects – I too, am a soldier!

Of the particulars of these glorious victories, we (being "out in the wilderness") have not been fully informed, but it is enough for us to know that we have gained them, and that too, by hard fighting. I wish you could have been in camp to day when the Col.'s Aids brought us a circular containing the news of the capture of Fort Donelson, Tennessee and Savannah, Georgia [Savannah was under siege but was not captured], with 15,000 prisoners, including Buckner, Johnson, and FLOYD. [The circular was not accurate. Johnson may refer to Gen. Albert S. Johnston who was not present at the battle of Fort Donelson, and Generals Pillow and Floyd escaped.]

The rain poured down in torrents, but nothing daunted, the different Regiments turned out *en masse* giving such cheers as made these grand hills fairly shake, and the old woods look astonished. But when Floyd's name was announced, the old 7th's cup of happiness was full. Of all the hoary traitors in Rebeldom – not excepting King

Jeff himself – we hold a special hatred to him. Who of us has forgotten Cross Lanes? Where is Dyer? – brave generous Dyer – and impetuous, lion-hearted Schutte? Sleeping their last quiet sleep on the banks of Meadow River. Where the brave boys with whom we have shared the long, weary march and the lonely bivouac? Fifteen fell with their faces to the foe and fill a soldier's grave. For the rest – go ask the polluted charnel houses of Richmond, Charleston, and New Orleans! Have we not good cause to remember this same Floyd – laying aside the fact of his being the Prince of Thieves and the vilest renegade running? But while the cause is making such glorious strides in the South, the "Right Wing of the Army of the Potomac" has not been entirely inactive. Gen. Lander is slowly extending his lines along the B. & O. R. R., driving the traitors before him at every step. His work is done quietly, and perhaps does not show as well in sensation columns as that of others, but its value is undoubted. The General is much beloved by his men, and appears to pursue his line of duty regardless of outside comment ...[12] [The remainder of the letter was about Tyler's move, the cavalry skirmish, and Capt. O'Brien's wounding, which were mentioned in the previous letter of D. G. S. This letter was signed FALSTAFF, which is another pseudonym.]

Camp Pawpaw, Va.,
Feb. 24, 1862.

Ed. Democrat:

Nothing since my last having occurred of note, or calculated in the least to interfere with the truthfulness of that stereotyped phrase of "All quiet on the Potomac," I will give you a brief account of the manner in which the 22d was observed in camp. Most of the day Friday was occupied in "fixing up," raising flag staffs and evergreen arches, decorating tents, burnishing muskets, scouring buttons, etc., preparatory to the great events of the morrow. In front of the field officers' quarters was a large and splendid arch hung with numerous wreathes of evergreens; in the center and reaching clear across in large green letters was the name *Washington,* over which waved the Star Spangled Banner. Noticeable also, in several of the company quarters of the Seventh, were fine arches and decorations with appropriate mottoes and inscriptions, but which is not necessary here to minutely describe. Suffice it to say, they were all gotten up in good style and reflected great credit upon the taste, ingenuity, and patriotism of the "getter upper."

The 22d dawned most gloriously and was ushered in by a National Salute from Daum's Battery and the "Star Spangled Banner" by the Seventh Regiment Band together with the other brass and martial bands of the camp – At 11 0'clock the Seventh Regiment was formed and marched to take its position on the right of the Third Brigade and was soon joined by the other regiments of the brigade: the 1st Virginia, 7th Indiana, 29th Ohio, 66th Ohio, and 110th Pennsylvania, when the whole was formed into line of battle. Then came dashing up the brigade cavalry, being detachments of the Ohio, Virginia, and Ringold Cavalry, headed by their splendid mounted band, and wheeled into line on the right and in rear of the infantry. Soon after, Gen. Tyler and his Aids having arrived on the ground, the order was given, "By right of companies rear into columns," and the parade began, and with six thousand bayonets glittering in the bright sunlight, the different regimental colors flying in the breeze, and the almost deafening sound of brass and martial music, interspersed with a little "sheet iron thunder" from Daum's Battery, the whole presented a spectacle extremely grand. After parading a short time, the column was again drawn up into line to await the arrival of Gen. Lander, whom I was understood, would be present and "discuss the important questions of the day." A salute from the infantry on our left soon announced his arrival, and in a few minutes the General and his Staff mounted on their splendid chargers, passed in front of and reviewed the column of infantry; after which they passed to the left and rear and reviewed the cavalry. After this had been gone through with, the parade was resumed and continued about an hour, when the column was formed into a solid mass and addressed by Gen. Lander. He said he was no speech maker but felt that he had something to say to the Third Brigade – He complimented the men for their soldierly bearing and the firmness with which they had stood up under their recent fatiguing marches. He also spoke of the late Union victories in Kentucky, Missouri, and Tennessee and proposed to march an army against equal numbers and gain a victory. He wanted every man to stand up to the work and not run as long as an officer was left to command; and if officers and all were killed, except one or two, then they could go home, tell the women they had seen some mighty good fighting, seen some good men killed, and had come home to help cry for them.

There was another thing to which he would call attention and that was the violation within the past few days of a general order respecting private property. Cases had come to his knowledge of hogs being killed, etc.; this he wanted stopped, and if the order was again violated, he would resort to hanging. – We had come here to fight for the Union and not to kill hogs; and low and degraded must be the soldier who would willfully and maliciously charge bayonet on a hog, and then dodge behind a stump to hide from his General. Not that he cared for the value of the hog, but general orders *must be obeyed.*

Col. Tyler then made a few brief and earnest remarks to the brigade, after which the parade was dismissed.

In the evening a large bonfire was built on the camp ground, around which a large crowd collected – the Band came out and discoursed some of their choicest music, and the festivities were kept up till a late hour. Thus ended the "doings" on the 22d at Camp Pawpaw on the "sacred soil."

Adjutant DeForest has resigned his commission and left camp this morning for Cleveland.

We are just now enjoying a "right smart" Virginia wind storm causing a general collapse of cotton. Several of the tents are down, and I expect ours will go next.

Very Respectfully,   D. G. S.
Co. A, 7th O.V. [13]

Camp Chase, Pawpaw, Va., B. & O. R.R.
March 7th, 1862.

Ed. Democrat:

One week ago today, just as we were starting off on a march from this Camp, I received your package of papers (12) of last week. We returned to camp Sunday evening somewhat fatigued, and since that time until to-day I have been very busy for Pay Day and attending to being paid off. We were paid yesterday by Pay-master Reese.

Previous to receiving the above mentioned package, I have received similar packages nearly every week since I have been in command of Co. G, but have neglected to acknowledge the receipt; but hoping you will pardon the neglect, I will for myself and the "boys" thank you for the kindness thus shown us, and be assured we shall ever be grateful for similar favors. Your paper is anxiously looked for, and its contents eagerly devoured when received, particularly the local department.

I distribute the packages among the Portage County "boys"

that they may get the home news.

We expect to move farther down in a day or two. – Part of the Division has already gone.

We are having nice Winter weather for the past few days, and we all hope it may remain so for a long time to come.

I look for your welcome paper by mail to-day.

Yours Truly,
SEYMOUR S. REED, Lieut.
Commanding Co. G., 7th O.V. [14]

In the March 12, 1862 edition of the *Democrat* there appears a whimsical piece that was acceptable at this stage of the war.

COL. TYLER'S PATRIOTIC MARCH – Prof. F. A. Eileman, the leader of the 7th Regiment Band, has arranged a brilliant piece of music which he has christened *Col. E. B. Tyler's Patriotic March*. Messrs. Brainard & Co. of Cleveland have published the music with an excellent and beautiful lithograph of Col. Tyler. Prof. Eileman is a musical genius, and one who has heard the Patriotic March discoursed by the 7th O.V. Band, pronounces it indeed a spirit-stirring piece of music and the handsome style in which it is published. [15]

Chapter Three

"I saw enough of the horrors of war"

Gen. Frederick W. Lander died from illness on March 2, 1862. Brig. Gen. James Shields, whose division was now part of the 5th Army Corps, succeeded Gen. Lander.

The Shenandoah Valley Campaign began on a positive note for the Union forces in the spring of 1862. Shield's Division, including the 7th Ohio, marched through Winchester toward Kerstown where they were attacked by Gen. Jackson's Confederate troops on March 23, 1862. Jackson received a tactical defeat and lost 718 men, whereas the Union loss was 568. [1]

Much was written then and ever since about the Battle of Kernstown, or Winchester; but this is how the battle appeared to Cpl. Wright of Co. G. Although the information regarding the larger scope of the battle is often inaccurate and probably based on hearsay, that should not detract from what Wright actually saw with his own eyes.

Washington Hotel, Newtown, Va.,
Tuesday, March 25, 1862.

Ed. Democrat: Since writing to you Friday last, we have had a hard-fought and bloody battle which terminated in the complete rout of the entire rebel force under generals Jackson, Longstreet, and Smith [Longstreet was not at Kernstown and there is not a prominent Smith mentioned.] – a glorious victory!

On Saturday afternoon last, the rebel Gen. Jackson, with his cavalry and artillery under command of Col. Ashby, drove in our pickets on the Strasburg road and commenced shelling the city. Gen. Shields with our cavalry, some artillery, and a regiment of infantry drove them back as far as this place, eight miles south of Winchester, when Jackson was reinforced. Our force then retired to Winchester to await the light of the next morning. Gen. Shields was wounded in the arm by the bursting of one of their shells which fell near him. Our brigade, under command of Col. Tyler, left camp three miles north of Winchester at sunset Saturday evening and marched into the city where we lay upon our arms all night ready for the rebel attack of the morrow. Gen. Banks with his division had the day previous moved out to Berryville pike to get in Jackson's rear, which he (Jackson) did "see into" – hence his boldness. [Banks was intending to withdraw to participate in Gen. McClellan's Peninsula Campaign. Jackson received reports of Bank's intentions and therefore made the attack on Shields to prevent Banks from joining McClellan. The strategy worked. [2]]

THE WINCHESTER BATTLE

About noon on Sunday, Jackson, who was now largely reinforced, again came up near the city and commenced an attack with shot and shell. Our artillery, supported by infantry and cavalry, now opened upon them a deadly fire. The rebel artillery was composed of thirty-two pieces, among which was Sherman's' battery captured at Manassas. We had four batteries – twenty-four pieces – under command of the brave Colonel Daum. The fire continued regularly on both sides for about five hours and was quite destructive. At four o'clock Col. Tyler told us he had been ordered to take a battery which was stationed to the right; and soon we were advancing by columns of divisions, the Seventh Ohio in front, under cover of the woods. When in the woods, we threw off our blankets and haversacks in piles in order to "go in on our nerve!" We silently advanced to the opening, when they opened a terrible volley upon us from their battery and the seven Virginia regiments supporting it. Terrible was the slaughter which now commenced on both sides. We soon silenced their battery, but the infantry having the advantage of us by being under cover of the woods, rocks, and a stone wall, held us for nearly an hour fighting like demons. Our reserve now came up and we drove them from rock to rock and from woods to woods capturing three of their pieces and about three hundred prisoners. Night setting in and darkness covering the battle-field, we ceased firing and rallied on a hill for the night.

THE BATTLE-FIELD, AT NIGHT

Sad was the scene, as with torches we gathered up the dead and wounded that night. The shrieks and groans of the wounded and dying even now ring in my ears. Here a man, with the top of his head shot off and his brains oozing out, still alive and begging to be shot; and there another with his limb shot off by a cannon ball, groaning in agony; and still another with both eyes shot out by a cross fire begging to have an end put to his misery. All night long were our ambulances running from the battle-field to Winchester, carrying the wounded to the hospitals.

THE DEAD

The dead, both Union and rebel, were gathered together in piles – numbering hundreds – to be buried on the morrow. As we straightened the limbs and folded the arms of the ghastly dead, we could not help but exclaim in the language of Burns –

"Peace, thy olive extend,
And bid wild war his ravage end;
Man with brother man to meet,
And as a brother kindly greet."

BRAVERY OF OUR OFFICERS.

During the engagement Col. Tyler and his Aids rode coolly along the line among us, cheering the men and giving orders. Lieut. Col. Creighton's horse was shot from under him, when he seized a musket and led his brave "roosters" (as he calls us) slowly but surely towards the foe. Major Casemate, whose overcoat has several bullet-holes through it, led a charge and took one of their big guns. Our noble Ensign carried the colors safely through, although two of his guard were wounded by his side. Between thirty and forty bullets riddled the flag, and the staff was cut away by a Minie ball.

"CLOSE CALLS"

Lieut. Quay, one of Col. Tyler's Aids, had his cap shot through, grazing the side of his head. Lieut. Searl of Company F also had his cap shot through without doing any damage. One of the boys was hit by a half spent ball, it going through his overcoat, blouse, vest, and "clean through" the miniature of "the girl he left behind him," where it stopped. Your humble servant was hit by a nearly spent ball just above the ankle which made him think of "the days when he was better off."

PURSUIT OF THE ENEMY

Yesterday at daylight, our batteries opened again upon the rebels who retreated, we following up, deploying as skirmishers to the right and left of the road, through woods and fields. Gen. Banks with part of his division, who had been sent for the previous evening, now came up to our support, and we moved on. When as far as this place, your humble servant's boots "played out," and he was ordered to "halt for reinforcement" of shoe leather! Our men were at dark last night as far as Cedar Creek, eight miles south from here and two miles this side of Strasburg. The enemy were in full retreat. They will not probably again make a stand until they reach Staunton. We shall go on to the regiment to-morrow.

NEWTOWN REBEL HOSPITAL

On Sunday night as the rebels retreated, they left what wounded they brought away – some twenty in number – at the church in this town in care of citizens. This morning we were up at the church conversing with some of them. When we told them that our surgeons had sent a great number of their wounded to Winchester, and that we had buried their dead, they were greatly surprised, having been told that we would kill their wounded and leave unburied their dead! One of them, a fine looking youth belonging to the 44th Virginia regiment, who was wounded in the shoulder, died while we were there. Another whose limb was shot entirely off, and remained on the battle-field will probably die during the day. The poor fellows admitted that they were fighting under the wrong banner, but the women (Heaven forgive them!) who were nursing them, declared that the Stars and Stripes had been disgraced and that *they* would never submit to us. They, perhaps, had better go into the field and fight against their own men when we shall have vanquished them! Newtown is a pretty little village of about a thousand inhabitants situated eight miles south of Winchester and ten miles north of Strasburg. It has furnished a company of cavalry and one of artillery for the Southern army.

UNION LOSSES

Our loss in killed and wounded will not exceed one hundred and fifty; while the rebels lost over three hundred in killed besides a large number of wounded. Col. Murray of the 84th Penn. was killed. Lieut. Williamson of the 29th Ohio, one of Col. Tyler's Aids was killed. Every company in our regiment suffered more or less. Orderly Sergeant Danforth of Co. C was shot through the head and killed instantly. John Fram of Co. G was shot through the bowels and died shortly afterwards. Sergeant Lazarus of Co. G was badly wounded in the face. Sergeant-Major Webb was dangerously wounded in the bowels. Capt. Burgess of Co. F and Capt. Asper of Co. H were both slightly wounded. Many others of our brave boys have slept their last sleep, and many are writhing in agony at the hospitals in Winchester. You will soon have a full report of the killed and wounded. A mounted brass band is now coming down the street discoursing to the citizens of Newtown that glorious old piece of music, "The Star Spangled Banner." The Fifth Connecticut and the Seventh New

Hampshire are coming into town. Hoping to date my next in Staunton or somewhere else in Dixie,

I remain yours respectfully,
D. H. W. [3]

The *Portage County Democrat* of Ravenna, Ohio was quite pleased and proud of the Union victory at Winchester, especially since Col. Tyler and the Portage County boys played such important roles. Col. Tyler received much favorable press, a sample of which follows.

With great satisfaction we record the gallant deeds of our Townsman, Col. Tyler, Acting Brigadier General, at the Battle of Winchester. All accounts verbal by returned soldiers and officers and published correspondence and official reports concur in pronouncing his bearing, on the hard fought field, brave and soldierly – and to the desperate charge made by his troops, himself at their head, in a great degree are we indebted for our decisive victory.

The Winchester correspondent of the New York Post in speaking of the charge, says, "The gallant TYLER led the charge, sword in hand, at the head of the line ... [Col. Kimball's official report says] Col. TYLER deserves the highest commendation for the gallant manner in which he led hid brigade during the conflict... [4]

The Seventh Ohio also received numerous encomiums under the following headlines and report.

THE WINCHESTER BATTLE !
The Day Won by Western Troops !
The Third Brigade First in the Fight !
The Gallant Seventh Covered With Glory !!

Lieut. E. S. Quay, A.A.A.G. of the 3rd brigade, Col. Tyler, arrived in Ravenna on Monday morning [March 31] direct from Winchester. He was accompanied by Adjutant Molyneaux of the 7th who proceeded to his home in Cleveland. These officers had with them the colors of the 7th which showed how gallantly our boys stood in the front of the battle, and how bravely they have again been baptised with fire and blood. The banner is punctured by twenty-eight bullet holes, the staff shot twice in two, the crescent and the tassel are left upon the battlefield to tell how heroically it was waved in the face of the foe. Color Sergeant Lawterwasser of the 7th kept his charge continuously aloft in the midst of the hottest fire, the fearful roll of artillery, and the death sent rattle of musketry. When the brave fellow could not keep his feet under the galling fire, he lay upon the ground and shook the banner at the foe...

The men and officers of the 7th did their duty well. Early in the engagement Lieut. Col. Creighton had his horse shot under him and he seized a musket and fought in the ranks. Maj. Casemate was among the bravest of the brave, with twenty men he stormed and took a brass cannon. The Major preserves a perforated coat as a trophy of this gallant deed. Adjt. Molyneaux did most excellent service, cool and intrepid through the whole and came out of the battle unharmed. Capt. J. M. Sterling of Company B fought like a hero, constantly cheering and pressing on his men. Capt. Asper fought most manfully, and as a reward for his valor was made a mark by a sharpshooter and received a severe flesh wound. Lieut. McClelland of Company I received a scalp wound, but bound a handkerchief about his head and stood his post. Lieut. Eaton, one Col. Tyler's Aids, had his horse shot from under him, but he was soon on another, attentive to the bidding of his chief. Col. Tyler rode the splendid bay he took from Ravenna last spring, and though in an exposed position came out unscathed. An officer of the signal corps, riding by the side of Col. Tyler, was struck upon a button by a spent ball, which he caught in his hands – a good catch, said he to Col. Tyler, and pocketed the trophy...[5]

The casualty lists for the Portage County boys lent a somber note to the euphoria of victory. The feverish patriotism and the pursuit of glory were somewhat dimmed when the names of the killed and ghastly wounded were posted. Lt. Reed of Company G not only confirmed his casualties but also let the home folks know who were in the battle and, indirectly, who were not in the fight.

Camp of the 7th Reg't. O.V.I.
Strasburg, Va., March 28th, 1862.

Ed. Democrat:

Undoubtedly long ere this, the news of the battle near Winchester on Sunday the 23d ult. has reached you and that the 7th Ohio acted a conspicuous part in said battle, being under and returning a hot fire for over two hours without moving the enemy, they holding their position until others came to the assistance of the brigade.

I understand that some of the men, who are members of Company G and under my command, are writing home claiming to have been in the battle, but who, I know, *were not*, and are thereby receiving praise and honor at home that is not due them.

That injustice may be done to none, and *justice* to those noble and gallant men who were with me in the battle and their friends at home, I send you an accurate list of those who were in the battle, and ask it as a favor that you publish the same, that Portage County people may know which of their gallant sons to be proud of.

Sergeants – George W. Barrett, James R. Loucks, Edward M. Lazarus, wounded in the face, Charles L. King.

Corporals – Harry M. Dean, Daniel W. Wright, Geo. A. Furry, Austin Bull, William T. Callow.

Privates – Clark E. Barnard, William R. Bond, James C. Bryon, Gilbert D. Bertholf, George K. Carl, William Cromwell, John Fram, killed, Samuel S. Fisher, Isaiah B. Green, Austin Hudson, George W. Houck, Franklin Harsh, Morris R. Hughes, Henry Howard, Martin Lazarus, Alfred E. May, Humphrey Owen, Israel Potts, James Pidgin, William H. Ripple, Arthur C. Stedman, Philip Smith, Zenas K. Smith, Jerry Wicks, Adam Woolf, Thomas Woolf, Thomas H. Whitmore.

I must say in justice to some whose names do not appear in the above list, that some in whom I have the utmost confidence, were sick and unable to go, and a few others were shoeless, and I was unable to obtain shoes for them, who were therefore left in camp.

Yours truly,

Seymour S. Reed, Lieut.,
Commanding Co. G, 7th Ohio [6]

The list for Company F was more extensive, as the *Democrat* reported on the old Franklin Rifles.

E. E. Tracy of Nelson was wounded "... pretty seriously in the left arm, just below the elbow. He is now at Winchester under good care. It is thought his arm can be saved.

G. Russell, also from Nelson, ... was slightly wounded in the back part of the head – just grazed by a ball.
Elias Hall, Brimfield, killed.
Moses Owen, Franklin, wounded.
Anson Pritchard, Franklin, wounded in the hip.
Fred Bethel, Franklin, wounded in the right shoulder.
Chas. W. Minnick, Franklin, wounded in the shoulder.
Edward Thompson, Nelso, right leg.
Captain Burgess, Nelson, leg.
Arby Twitchell, Brimfield, hand.

From a private letter dated March 25, 1862, the *Democrat* quoted the writer as follows. "... I was on the battlefield soon after the fight. The sight there was awful – perfectly horrible to look upon. As I saw the haggard, ghastly, upturned faces of the dead, my heart sickened at the sight. – We counted thirty-six corpses of the secesh, and did not see the third part of them. I saw enough of the horrors of war..." [7]

The Portage County boys now received a respite from the forced marches and heavy fighting. They had time to admire the spring weather and the scenery in the Shenandoah Valley. News of victories elsewhere in addition to their own recent success further enlightened the hope that nature brings in the Springtime.

Camp Near Edinburg, Va.,
Friday, April 4th, 1862.

Editor Democrat: As an opportunity of sending letters to "Old Portage," through the kindness of Col. H. L. Carter, is now to be had, a few lines as to our whereabouts are herewith sent you.

We are now camped on the East side of the Manassas Gap Railroad, one mile North of the town of Edinburg, four miles South of Woodstock, the county seat of Shenandoah county, and seventeen miles South of Strasburg. We left Strasburg on Tuesday morning, arriving here the same afternoon, shelling the rear guard of Gen. Jackson, (Ashby's Cavalry and Artillery) as we came. Gen. Jackson is at Mt. Jackson six miles further up the valley, which place is the terminus of the Manassas Gap Railroad. The hospitals there are said to be filled with many of their men who were wounded at the late battle of Winchester. What a pity this, the lovely valley of Virginia, should be the scene of bloody carnage as it has already been and soon will be again, unless the reckless Jackson "digs out" immediately.

Our men are engaged in building a bridge across Strong Creek, just at the upper end of town, which Ashby fired in his retreat, and when that is finished "onward we will go." Gen. Shields, the brave old hero and Irish patriot, our present leader, is among us, although suffering considerably from the wound received at Winchester a short time since. – Our wounded are being kindly cared for at the hospitals in Winchester. The number of killed and wounded from the Seventh Ohio Regiment in the late battle of Winchester was nearly *one hundred*!

Capt. F. A. Seymour arrived in camp to-day bringing several letters from our friends at home. The Democrat of the 26th ult., in its neat and tasty, new dress has been received. The weather is delightful, and the "boys" are again ready to meet Gen. Jackson and his "Stonewall brigade." Letters will reach the Seventh Ohio by being directed to the Third Brigade, Shield's Division, via Winchester. Respectfully,

D. H. W. [8]

Edinburg, Va., April 16th, 1862.

Ed. Dem.: -- Nothing of vast importance has occurred in this portion of the Army of the Potomac since the battle of Winchester, of which I gave you a brief account in my last. Our column is now encamped at this place, situated some eighteen miles South-West from Strasburg and 8 miles North of Mount Jackson, on the Manassas Gap Rail Road, and near a "babbling brook" which bears the name of Stony Creek. Edinburg is a village which before the breaking out of war could have boasted of a population of 1,000; but that number has been greatly reduced and at present will not exceed 400, principally *women and children* – the "men folks" having gone to fight for their country under the *Stars* and *Bars*.

The rebels have one or two batteries planted on an open hill on the opposite side of the river, and amuse themselves by throwing an occasional shell at us. But a few doses of "cast iron thunder" from our batteries serves to convince them that there is still work for them to do. The enemy's pickets and ours are in sight of each other, and it is not infrequent that shots are exchanged. Should this state of affairs continue, it is not unlikely that *somebody will get hurt*. The enemy's force across the river is not supposed to be large.

I have wondered why we remain here so long; but when I reflect that we belong to the *Army of the Potomac*, perhaps the thing needs no better explanation. We must necessarily keep a little "quiet."

Intelligence of the great Union victories at Pittsburg Landing [Shiloh] and Island No. 10 [on the Mississippi River] has been received here, and occasioned the greatest enthusiasm.

The Regimental Colors of the 7th have returned, on which has been inscribed in golden letters: "Winchester, March 23d, 1862."

Bang! bang! bang! Helloa, the artillery has opened again. It is probably our fellows shelling the rebels across the river. I must go and see.   D. G. S.
Co. A, 7th O.V. [9]

Strasburg, Va., April 19, 1862.

Ed. Democrat: -- Since our sojourn in Dixie and especially in this part of it, I have had ample opportunities to look upon the ravages of this war, and learn the feelings of many of the inhabitants of the Upper Valley of Virginia in regard to it. As a general thing, the inhabitants who had been the rankest Secessionists lost all hope when they saw Jackson's celebrated army flying from us, utterly routed on the field of Winchester.

They felt that secession was indeed a terrible failure here. And they now acknowledge that they have been deceived. The horde of vandals which were to sweep down upon them from the countless swarms of the North, free their slaves, burn their towns and villages, and spread terror and devastation everywhere were indeed men, well behaved, well disciplined, well fed, and well clothed. They found an army which had come among them to bring law and order instead of terror and confusion.

They were surprised, for they had been taught for a twelve-month by the minions of Davis, that the march of the Yankees into the territory of Virginia was but the signal for their subjugation.

Many of the Southern soldiers are now coming back to their homes, perfectly satisfied if they can only reach them. A large part of them were enlisted for only one year, and I am told by those having sons in the Southern ranks that they expected to come home at the expiration of that time.

But strong inducements are held out to then to re-enlist. Furloughs for forty days were given to all who would do so. Some again enlisted for two years or the war. But others refused to do so. – in fact, a large proportion preferring to forego the opportunity of going home on furlough, as well as run the risk of being drafted, rather than pledge themselves again to service. But soon after this order for drafting was issued, it was followed by another compelling *every* man between the ages of 18 and 45 to enroll themselves for service. Thus those who had hoped to return to their homes were faced by the proposition to volunteer on the one hand or be certainly drafted on the other.

A hard alternative, indeed, but one which they were compelled to accept.

AN INCIDENT

A few days since, a fire broke out in town and threatened to consume a dwelling house occupied by an elderly matron, who, as it happened, was one of the most ultra in regard to the doctrine of secessia – in fact, a zealous disciple of Jeff. Nearly all the male inhabitants were in the Southern army, but present help was needed or all the old lady's earthly possessions would soon be amongst the things that were. Col. Moody of the 66th O.V., commander of the post, with his gallant boys was soon hard at work. And soon the flames were extinguished and nearly everything saved. The old lady stood by, and with every feature lighted up with joy that it was so well with her, exclaimed, "God bless our enemies! how they work!" Truly, for once at least, she fulfilled the gospel injunction, "Love your enemies."

Fifty of Ashby's celebrated cavalry were taken prisoners day before yesterday at Columbia Furnace, about twenty miles from here. They passed through here this morning on the way to Baltimore. The greater part of them were very young, not more than 18 or 20 years of age.

The troops are almost wild with joy occasioned by the success of our arms in the West and South. The capture of Island No. 10 is considered the most brilliant exploit of the war among military men here. The news of the battle of Pittsburg Landing and the fall of Fort Pulaski was received with exultation.

The army pulse is stronger, and the weight of care seems to be lifted from us, which seemed to press us down with uncertainty and doubt before our victories began.

The weather a week ago was cold, snowy, and freezing –

now, as hot as July in Ohio. The peach trees are now in full blossom and apple trees leafing out – although I am told that the season is one month later than usual this Spring.

CORNELIUS [10]

New Market Va.,
April 29th, 1862.

Ed. Democrat: -- Gen. Shield's Division is now encamped in and about this place, while the remainder of Banks' command are still further out on the Staunton road, the whole column having advanced from Edinburg on the 16th. Jackson on his retreat attempted to burn all the bridges in his rear in order to impede our progress; but we generally arrived to extinguish the flames before any serious damage had been done. Jackson had intended to make a stand just this side of Mt. Jackson, and for that purpose had his force drawn up in line of battle, but upon discovering our men advancing also in line of battle, he concluded it would be better to postpone it till some other time. It is generally believed that Jackson has escaped over the mountains and is making his way in direction of Gordonsville.

The present camp ground of the Third Brigade is a fine one, situated about two miles South from New Market, and battalion drills and dress parade are again the order of the day.

The news of Tyler's appointment as a Brigadier has [been] received here with general satisfaction, all agreeing that it was *the right man in the right place.*

We have just received intelligence of the capture of New Orleans. Cannons are booming, bands are playing, and [it] commands general enthusiasm.

Yours respectfully,
D. G. S.
Co. A., 7th Reg't. [11]

It was customary for the *Portage County Democrat* to exhibit the poetic talents of local contributors on the front page of the newspaper. This April 30th contribution lauded the sacrifice of the 7th Ohio.

TO THE BANNER OF THE HEROIC SEVENTH
By Mrs. T. G. Springer

Glorious Banner! Soiled and torn,
Through the battle proudly flying,

Gallant hands have thee up-borne,
Hands beneath the sod now lying;
Through the gathering mists of Death
Eyes have brightened to behold thee!

Screaming shot, nor murderous shell,
Ne'er a moment made thee falter,
Waving high o'er those that fell
Sacrificed on Freedom's altar;
Glorious Banner! Ever live
Shrined in song and famed in story!
Hero hearts their worship give
To those colors bathed in glory.

Stricken wife, thine orphan bring,
On that ensign gaze with pride;
Teach them, more than knight or king
Was their sire who 'neath it died;
Mourning mother, lift thy brow, --
The brave boys that you have given,
With their sheaves of honor, now
Stand beside the throne of Heaven.

O, my country, racked and torn!
Fear not – truth will be victorious;
Traitor hordes, of darkness born,
Flee before our arms so glorious;
Soon shall war and carnage cease,
Slavery from its throne be hurled,
And beneath the wings of Peace
All our banners shall be furled. [12]

The available Union troops out-numbered Gen. Jackson's Confederate troops by approximately four to one; however, the Federal Army in the Shenandoah Valley was poorly coordinated. Jackson attacked them in detail and won victories at McDowell on May 8, Front Royal on May 23, Winchester on May 25, Cross Keys on June 8, and Port Republic on June 9. In short, the Union forces were out-generaled, out-marched, and out-fought by Gen. Thomas Jonathon Jackson and his "foot cavalry." Through this chain of events the Union troops in the Shenandoah Valley were prevented from joining Gen. Irvin McDowell near Washington, D.C.; and Jackson prevented the the proposed linking of McDowell's forces with those of McClellan's which were at the gates of Richmond. After this performance of Jackson, the disdain for the Confederate commander, which appeared in the letters of Pvt. Stein and the other correspondents, was replaced by a newfound respect for "Stonewall" in the following letters.

Somewhere in Rockingham Co., Va.,
Tuesday Morning, May 6th, 1862.

Ed. Dem.: -- Having just finished a *sumptuous* repast of coffee, hard bread and meat, and having disposed of ourselves in a peculiar military "posish," sitting tailor fashion on mother earth, under a pile of rails, we write to you, "and hope these few lines will find you *enjoying* the same blessing."

OUR PRESENT LOCALITY.

As nearly as we can calculate, the Third Brigade is now encamped five miles South of New Market and ten miles North of Harrisonburg in the County of Rockingham. Yesterday at this time, we were encamped further up the valley, but for some reason we fell back to this spot – probably a ruse. Our artillery are posted on the two hills to our right and left, and we are anxiously awaiting an attack from "Old Stonewall," who has been largely reinforced and who threatens to "clean out" Banks and Shields. Hope he will "try it on."

A SOLDIER'S LIFE.

Thinking perhaps a few items in the life of a "bould sojer," how he "puts in his time," and what he carries on a march, might prove of interest to the myriad readers of your valuable and interesting paper, we will here give them.

DAILY ROUTINE.

The first thing in the morning is a tune from the "sheepskin band," called Reveille, which awakens the sleepy "soger boy," whether he would or no, and begins to pick himself up, preparatory to being summoned by the Orderly Sergeant to "Fall in to Roll Call!" which is soon done, when he "piles out" in a hurry and gets into line with his comrades to escape being "pricked" and put on guard, which is the penalty for non-appearance at roll call. When roll call is over, with soap and towel in hand he "lights out" for the nearest creek, pool, spring, river, or mud hole, as the case may be, to perform his toilet. – This done, he returns to his tent, when breakfast is announced. You enter the tent, "Sibley," and look around. The "soger" and his messmates are seated Turk fashion, with hard bread in hand, tin plates having long since "played out," and a tin cup, awaiting the arrival of the mess cook with his cauldron of coffee and mess-pan of fried pork or beef, when the onslaught is made, and shortly after the *"good things"* (!) have disappeared, and breakfast is over. Surgeon's call is now beat, and the "lame, halt, and blind" hobble out to the Hospital where quinine is dosed out to each, no matter what his complaint! Next comes "Guard Mounting." At the signal from the Cornet Band, the Guards are paraded before the Officer of the Day and marched off to relieve the Guards of the previous day. Company drill of an hour or two is next announced by the "never silent drum," when our rusty old muskets are brought out and rubbed up a little so as to look respectable, and soon we are racking around the drill ground at common, quick, and double-quick time, going through unheard of evolutions. This over, we return to our quarters, where perhaps a kettle of beans await our arrival, before being "collapsed," which is also done on the double-quick style. Dinner is now over, and we go out under the shade of some tree for a little snooze or to write a letter, and just as we get into the merits of the case, that drum says: "Get ready for Battalion drill!" If we have but a few finishing touches to give our letter or a few more snores to give our snooze, no matter, we drop all, bundle on our "harness," seize our musket, fall into line, and await "further orders." – Soon, our Colonel, mounted on his white charger, appears and gives the proper order, when in less time than it takes me to tell it, we are drawn up in line of battle! Another order, and we are in the form of a hollow square to resist cavalry, and still another and we are in columns of divisions, and so on. – Drill over, we return to quarters and eat our little rations of hard bread, meat, and coffee which is erroneously called supper! And another call, and we brush up our hair, clothes, and "brogans" preparatory for dress parade. At dress parade, the band parades before the regiment playing the "Star Spangled Banner," "Out of the Wilderness," "The Girl I Left Behind Me," "Yankee Doodle," "Dixie," or some other march or quickstep, "as the case may be;" and several formalities are gone through, throughout which the field and line officers figure most conspicuously, showing their "good clothes and *handsome* proportions to an advantage. The orders for the next being read by the Adjutant, the parade is dismissed. The next call of the drum (the most agreeable of the whole day) announces the arrival of the mail. How eagerly the "boys" gather around the Orderly to receive their letters with happy expectant countenances, and how chop-fallen he looks who receives no kind word from friends at home. We would here say, for the benefit of such, to their friends at home, write often, write cheerful, give all the news, fill at least two sheets of letter paper, leave no cold blank spots, and if you cannot tell it all then, write crossways of the sheet. Good, kind, cheerful words from absent friends to the soldier helps him to endure his hard- ships, strengthens his power to resist evil temptations, and prevents *ennui*. Again we say, write often. From Retreat until Tattoo, the "boys" write, sing, play chess, checkers, whist, euchre, or sleep, as their inclinations lead them; when there is a general bed-making which consists in spreading out a handful of straw or brush, and over that their blankets, the knapsack serving as a pillow. Soon all are in bed, and at the last beat of the drum, "taps," the lights are extinguished and all is still save the heavy tread of the alarm guard as he walks his lonely beat.

KNAPSACKS.

As the soldier carries from place to place his "bed and board," you may ask in what does he carry it, and how much? – We will take our knapsack, for that is the name of the institution in which we carry our bed, wardrobe, etc., and examine it. With one or two exceptions it will represent the majority of knapsacks. In it we find an overcoat, dress-coat, two shirts, three pairs of socks, two handkerchiefs, a quantity of paper and envelopes, a Testament, and a case of homeopathic medicine, (for we are our doctor!) and on the outside, or top, rather, are fastened by means of straps and buckles, two blankets, one woolen and the other rubber. What a load! You say – but this isn't half that we have to carry!

HAVERSACKS.

Our little ration of hard bread, meat, coffee, etc., is carried in a sack known by the above name. It is capable of holding three days rations. Let us examine the interior of this "traveling pantry." We find eighteen or twenty "*hard*-breads," a poke of ground coffee, a little of sugar, a good-sized piece of "dead hog," a bottle (!) nothing but vinegar in it, however, and a box of grated radish. With a small tin cup, usually strapped on the outside, and combined knife, fork, and spoon carried in a pocket, (and a truly Yankee invention it is,) you have a complete description of our outfit in the commissary department!

PREPARING FOR A MARCH.

At the order to prepare for a march, knapsacks are packed, blankets rolled up, haversacks filled, muskets stacked in line, tents "collapsed," rolled up, and with kettles, mess pans, stoves, etc., packed into wagons, and when our cartridge boxes, which hold forty rounds, knapsacks, haversacks, canteens, etc., are put on, and our gun in hand, our outfit is complete, and we are ready for the march.

ON THE MARCH.

Soon we are on the march, sometimes through mud and water, especially in Winter time, and sometimes almost blinded by a cloud of dust, in which case we eat our "peck of dirt" all at one time; we plod our way along through the country from camp to camp. – Except in cases of forced marches, occasional rests are ordered, when you ought to see the "boys" make for the fence-corners or in the shade of some friendly tree, and there on their backs, lolling like a tired hound-pup, *enjoying* themselves for a few moments, when the word "fall in" is given and on they go again. In conclusion, we would say in the language of the "poeck;"

"Johnny! Would you go for a Sojer boy"
Respectfully,
Your ob't serv't,
D. H. W.
Co. G, 7th O.V. [13]

Pvt. Wright continued to educate the home folks in an interesting and entertaining fashion in his next letter. Meanwhile, Stonewall Jackson's "boys" were marching hard with little time to educate their folks back home.

Picket Post, Four Miles From Camp,
Saturday Noon, May 10th, 1862.

Editor Democrat: -- This beautiful day finds Company G on picket duty again. – We left camp four miles North of here at nine o'clock this morning and arrived here at ten, and relieved Company B which came out yesterday morning. The Seventh is still encamped five miles South of New Market, as when last I wrote. Yesterday, the tents of the Third Brigade, excepting those of the field and line officers, were taken from us, probably for some wise purpose, and we are now bivouaced in our little "seven-by-nine" Poncho tents!

PICKET DUTY.

As the *strangest* of strange ideas are formed in regard to picket duty by our civilian friends at home, perhaps a description of said duty may prove of some interest to your readers. Each morning the picket guard, consisting of one company each from the different regiments forming the Brigade, is paraded at head-quarters and then marched off through the woods and fields to some out-of-the-way place, the last company in line taking the nearest post to Camp, and the first taking the outpost four miles South of the Camp. The Companies are generally stationed at distances of a mile apart and so divided that there is one continual line of communication of the outpost with the Camp. In case of an attack, the different squads of a Company meet at the previously designated rallying post and if possible maintain their position until the Camp is sufficiently alarmed and put in "fighting attitude!" Each Brigade, forming a division, send out their pickets upon the different roads and lanes leading to the Camp, and it is thus strongly guarded on all sides. During the night, the different squads are so arranged as to relieve each other, a part sleeping while the others watch and wait for the appearance of the artful and wily enemy! Such is picketing.

REBEL DESERTER.

A young man belonging to Capt. White's Guerilla Band, organized in Louden county, came in this morning and gave himself up. He reported Generals Jackson, Ewell, and Johnson, thirty thousand strong, between Harrisonburg and Gordonsville. He said that out of his Company, which started out with sixty men in December last, *only fifteen remained*, the rest having deserted! He also reported that Capt. White and Col. Ashby were lying at the point of death from fever. None of his Company had received one cent pay, as yet, for their services and all were heartily tired of the business. [Author's note: The deserter was highly misinformed or else he was a plant put there by the wily Jackson.]

UNCLE HORACE.

Uncle Horace, an intelligent old darkee belonging to widow Thomas, who lives just below here, has just now come up from an adjoining field and the following conversation ensues: Good morning, Uncle!" "Good mornin, good mornin, gentlemun!" "How old are you uncle?" "Dunno, dun' no, sir; bin long time since I cum from over de Blue Ridge." "Where is your master?" "My ole massa, he's gone whar we'll all go soon; massa died six year dis cummin summer." –

"What do you think of this war, uncle?" "Berry bad ting, dis war; ole Horace tole 'em so, 'fore dey begun." "Why did the South rebel, uncle Horace?" "Cos Mr. Jeff. Davis tole 'em to, I reckon!" We think old uncle Horace's wooly "head is level!"

THE FRUIT.

A more flattering prospect for an abundance of fruit never before presented itself. The apple, peach, and cherry trees are fairly smothered with blossoms. The wheat fields are looking fine and promise a rich harvest. – What few farmers there are left, are just beginning to plant their corn. Capt. Seymour, the same jovial "jolly old soul" as ever, is well and in fine spirits. It is thought we will start on a "big march" in a day or two, probably to reinforce McDowell. Hoping to date my next in Richmond, I remain,

Respectfully,   D. H. W. [14]

Near Warrenton, Fauquier Co., Va.,
Sunday Morning, May 18th, 1862.

Editor Democrat: To-day, the sixth day of our "big march" finds us one mile south-east of Warrenton, bivouaced in a shady wood. We will probably go on as far as Warrenton Junction, nine miles to the south-east, this afternoon. The weather is delightful, and the "boys" are in fine spirits, all eager to join McDowell.

OUR "BIG MARCH."

Early on Monday morning last, the pickets being called in and breakfast over, the three brigades forming Shield's Division left their camp five miles south of New Market, Rockingham county, and commenced their march to join McDowell at Fredericksburg. At seven o'clock we were on the move, the Seventh Ohio, a squadron of cavalry, and a section of Daum's artillery acting as rear guard. When down the valley as far as New Market we took the road to Luray, Page county, crossing the Shenandoah range through Massanutton Gap. The road through the gap is very winding and rocky, and reminded us of our pilgrimage through Western Virginia last summer. At about sunset we crossed the south and main branch of the Shenandoah, through a long covered bridge, and bivouaced at a small place called Hamburg two miles west of Luray. Six miles over a mountain and in the midst of a dense cloud of dust we marched on this our first day. As our tents had been taken from us, the knapsacks were carried in the wagons. Early the next morning, (Tuesday), we were on the move. At Luray we took the Luray and Front Royal Turnpike for Front Royal and after a slow march of twelve miles, again halted and bivouaced. The day was sultry and the dense cloud of dust almost intolerable. It now commenced raining which was a most agreeable change for awhile, but after raining all night, the *agreeable* became "played out" in our estimation! The next day (Wednesday), we plodded our way through the stickiest of sticky mud, sixteen miles to Front Royal at which place we arrived at three o'clock P.M. All day the rain poured down in torrents and we were completely drenched. Our road was very winding and hilly, some-times it lay along the lovely Shenandoah, being walled on the oppo-site side by high perpendicular bluffs, and sometimes it wound up among the hills two and three miles from the river. Marching through town we bivouaced one mile out on the road to Gaines Cross Roads. This was a weary march and the "boys" were pretty much "played out." The next morning (Thursday), after sleeping at the rate of "fifty knots an hour" in spite of the continued rain, we moved slowly over the Blue Ridge through Chestnut Gap. The mountain and valley scenery from this gap, looking to the south-east, has an incredible grandeur! Peak after peak of the grand old Blue Ridge looms up until lost in the blue of the distance. In the valley beyond we came across Jim and Sam, two jolly specimens of "Old Virginia," belonging to a widow lady near Warrenton, but were hired to a farmer here, who informed us that five hundred secesh cavalry, under Col. Munson, had a few hours previous "gone ober to tar up de track an' burn the railroad bridge." Soon skirmishers were deployed to the right and left of the road in the quest of these "bould cavaliers," but none were found, and we moved slowly on. This day only nine miles were made as it still continued to rain, and our long train of wagons, heavily loaded, was consequently slow in its progress. Again we bivouaced and scraped *the everlasting mud* from our Government "brogans." Thus ended the fourth day. On Friday we made the "slowest time on record," going only *eight* miles! Raining as "usual!" Mud, pretty well *mixed*! Passing through the little village of Flint Hill we reached Gaines Cross roads, where signs of "the inimy" were plain. – Cavalry and infantry skirmishers were sent out and a slight skirmish ensued. Two of our cavalrymen were wounded, also two horses. Three of the rebels "bit the dust," and two were taken prisoners, when the rest "lit out" in hot haste. At Gaines Cross Roads lives a wealthy farmer by the name of Fletcher. He has thirty-five hundred acres of land in a body, fifty slaves, and hires one hundred workmen the year around. His mansion and negro-quarters are built of brick, and (thank Heaven!) the rain ceased. Yesterday morning we arose "bright and early" and at eight o'clock with a full haversack, a clear sky over our heads, and a good pike under our feet, we started for Warrenton. At noon we forded the Rappahannock river, the bridge being destroyed by the rebels. Two large steam woolen factories that had turned out thousands of woolen blankets for the Southern army were passed, and at five o'clock P.M. we came in sight of the handsome, wealthy town of Warrenton. Soon after we bivouaced (eighteen miles from where we had started in the morning) in these woods.

LURAY.

This town through which we passed is the county seat of Page, and contains a population (not in war times) of one thousand, white and black. It is a handsome place having several fine and costly residences.

FRONT ROYAL.

This town, situated just west of the Blue Ridge on the Manassas Gap railroad, is the county seat of warren and has about one thousand inhabitants. Two large military hospitals, built for the accommodation of the rebel wounded at Bulls Run, are located here. The town is nearly surrounded by high hills upon which is grown in considerable quantities the grape.

WARRENTON.

This town of Warrenton is the gayest, handsomest, and wealthiest place we have seen since coming into Virginia. It has a population of about three thousand. The residences are of the most costly character. The residence of Congressman "Extra Billy" Smith, of Congressional notoriety, is a model of elegance and southern taste. Over one hundred of the Bull Run wounded are buried here. The place is connected by a branch railroad of ten miles with the Virginia Central at Warrenton Junction. The streets, as we came through town, were crowded with handsome ladies and well dressed negro servants. Our band played "The Red, White, and Blue," and one lady (!) at the sight of the colors, covered her face with her delicate hands and didn't weep! The indications are that at no distant day we may be permitted to return to our homes. Rebellion is on its "last legs." Letters should be divided in order to reach us; -- Company -- 7th Ohio Reg., Third brigade, Shield's Division, via Washington.

Most respectfully,
D. H. W. [15]

The *Democrat*'s edition of June 4, 1862 reported the death of one of its earlier correspondents.

Murder of Dr. I. S. King.

The murder of Dr. Ira Selby King of this village, a volunteer in Co. G, 7th Regiment, was murdered [sic] at Winchester on the 24th of May at the time the rebels occupied the place. Dr. King has been in the Medical Department of the 7th a long time – and at this time was Hospital Steward. L. J. Clark of Co. H, 7th Regiment, gives this account of the murder of Dr. King. The hospital building was fired upon and set on fire by the rebels. Surgeon Salter of the 7th was wounded in the leg, two women from Ohio, nurses, were killed, and also Dr. King – who it is said rushed out of the hospital to take in a sick or wounded man, when he was shot in the leg, but taking in the sick man, he attempted to go out of the rear door, when a rebel shot him in the breast and he fell dead. Dr. King is the second son of Gen. John B. King of Ravenna – whose third son is also in the Union army.

His blood cries for vengeance. Shall longer probation be meted out to ruffians who fire hospitals and murder women? But this is the price of loyalty – the reward for devotion to the country. – Where ought we to stop, short of the extermination of these merciless assassins?

Dr. King was twenty-nine years of age – was born and passed all his days in Ravenna. His wife and orphans – little Georgie and Carrie – together with his father's family, share deeply in the tender and most heart-felt sympathy of the entire community. [16] [This article must have added to the extreme grief of the King family; and the report surely had propaganda value. However, better news awaited the grieving King family and the Ravenna community. Dr. Ira King was taken prisoner at Winchester, not killed. He was later paroled. Eventually, Dr. King was discharged for disability on April 15, 1864.]

Gen. Tyler's brigade played a major role in the battle of Port Republic. Tyler selected a good position between the South Fork of the Shenandoah River on his right and the Blue Ridge on his left. Although his three thousand man force was out-numbered by at least four to one by the combined Confederate forces. Tyler's brigade put up a stiff resistance and was able to repulse a frontal assault. The Union forces were aggressive and advanced. They were then attacked on their left flank by Gen. Ewell, while Gen. Richard Taylor was taking all but one of the artillery guns on the Union left by shooting all of the horses. The Union line broke, and a precipitate retreat down the valley ensued.

Following the battle of Port Republic, there is a noticeable drop in the soldier correspondence from the 7th Ohio Regiment to the *Portage County Democrat*. The pseudonyms of "Everett," "Cornelius," and "Falstaff" are not heard from again. Perhaps, they were casualties in the valley campaign.

Gen. Tyler's official report, dated June 12, 1862, was printed on the front page of the *Democrat* on June 25th. Lt. Col. Creighton's report, dated June 14th, appeared in the newspaper on July 9th. Both reports presented the details of the battle and emphasized the positive aspects of the performance of their men. Gen. Tyler wrote: "The loss of the enemy must have been very heavy. The grape and cannister from our batteries and the fire of our musketry mowed them down like grass before a well-served scythe" For heroic gallantry, Tyler cited Col. Creighton and six others as being among the bravest in the U. S. Army. Col. Creighton remarked: "The regiment left the field in good order, and throughout the whole retreat behaved in a most soldierlike manner. I cannot too highly praise the conduct and gallant bearing of the officers and commanders of the different companies of my regiment."

In Companies F and G alone, there were twenty-four men listed as killed, wounded, or missing. Their names appeared on the front page of the *Democrat*'s June 18th edition.

> Killed And Wounded Of Co's F. And G. 7th Regiment, At The Battle Of Port Republic – Capt. E. S. Quay, of Gen. Tyler's staff, arrived in Ravenna on Tuesday morning [June 17] – from him we have the following list of killed, wounded, and missing of the Portage County Companies of the 7th – which will be read with interest – and the apprehension of friends for others than those named will be thus relieved.
>
> Co. F. – Leroy M. Chapman, Brimfield, wounded in the head. Left on the field, wound probably mortal.
>
> Lieut. A. H. Day, Franklin, wounded in the left shoulder and neck.
>
> Lawrence Remel, wounded in the neck.
>
> Corp. M. V. Burt, Brimfield, wounded in the left arm

(the ball entered the Diary carried in his breast pocket, and thereby was prevented from entering the body.)
  A. W. Morely, wounded in the leg.
  Corp. Cyrus DeLong, wounded in the leg.
  Sylvester Matthews, wounded in the leg.
  W. H. Johnson, missing.
  Co. G, -- Corp. Julius Ruoff, Ravenna, killed.
  Albert Steadman, killed, shot through the breast.
  Boynton Lewis, Ravenna, killed, shot through the lungs.
  Seargt. J. R. Louck, Ravenna, wounded in the right hip, -- dangerously.
  Seargt. Chas. L. King, Ravenna, wounded in the face – probably mortal.
  Frank Eldridge, Edinburg, wounded in the thigh – not dangerous.
  Marion Hoover, wounded in both thighs.
  Wm. W. Rogers, Parkman, wounded in the head – probably mortal.
  Geo. O. Geylin, Rootstown, wounded in the head.
  Geo. R. Carl, Edinburg, wounded in the right arm, small bones fractured, but not bad.
  Harry H. Dean, Ravenna, wounded slightly by a spent ball in the leg.
  Ira Herrick, wounded slightly in the hand.
  H. M. Holton, taken prisoner.
  Horatio N. Hansen, taken prisoner.
  Benton Merrill, missing.
  Tod Hughes, missing.
  All the dead were left on the field and the wounded taken to Luray, Page County, Va., -- where the regiment was encamped on Thursday [June 12]. [17]

Chapter Four

"like grass before the mower"

Daniel H. Wright received the joy of a summer furlough to the folks back home. To the observant young soldier, his return to Portage County, Ohio was an educational and sight-seeing journey. However, this idyllic interlude proved to be the serene calm before another raging storm.

"Wildwood," June 20, 1962.

Ed. Dem: -- This clear and pleasant afternoon finds your humble servant at his "father's house," which is pleasantly situated in the Township of Freedom, County of Portage, and State of Ohio, and (thank Heaven!) far away from Dixie! The pleasures and comforts of Home, to the returned "sojer boy," prompts the following from the sensible pen of some one:
"Home! Home, sweet Home!
There's no place like Home!"
HOW WE OBTAINED A FURLOUGH.

As you must know, ere this, Shield's Division has for the last five weeks "been on a tramp," marching during that time nearly *four hundred miles*! And then, "weary and worn, sick and sore," part of it engaged "Old Stonewall" at Port Republic and was compelled, after nearly five hours terrible fighting, to retire, leaving Jackson in possession of the field. About a week previous to the battle, we had the misfortune to sprain the ankle joint, and after marching *one hundred miles* to Port Republic, re-sprained it. This was not enough yet; so we "wiggles along" *forty miles* back to Luray with the regiment. – Here we had the good fortune to get a certificate of disability from the Surgeon, a furlough from the Captain, Colonel, and general, and on Thursday evening we were on our way to the land of plenty – the Old Buckeye State!
OUR TRIP HOME.

Leaving Luray, Page County, Va., upon Thursday evening in a four-horse army wagon, we rode all night on the worst of roads, now at one end of the vehicle, and by a sudden jolt, we find ourselves the next moment at the other end, rubbing our bruised cranium. Thus we reached the railroad depot at Front Royal at nine o'clock Friday morning. Here we received a pass from the Provost Marshal to Washington, and at noon we were under way. At sunset we reached the famous battle-grounds of Manassas and Bull's Run, and later in the night, about ten o'clock, we halted at Alexandria.

Bright and early Saturday morning, we were whirling along the banks of the broad Potomac toward Washington, and after crossing this lovely river on the celebrated Long Bridge, we found ourselves in the Capital of the United States. At three o'clock in the afternoon, we were on our way to the great city of Baltimore, which place we reached at five o'clock P.M. After partaking of a "tip-top" supper at the City Hotel, No. 30 Bath Street, and taking a short ramble down [the] street, we left the Monumental City for Harrisburg, the Capital City of the old Keystone State, where we arrived at 3:30 on Sunday morning. As there was "no use of talking," about going any further that day, we tried to make the best of it by putting up at the well-ordered City Hotel, No. 128 Market Street, where we remained until the next morning at three o'clock, when we were off for Pittsburg. The traveler over this route from Harrisburg to Pittsburg of 250 miles, must (unless he be lost to all appreciation) enjoy the lovely scenery. Now he swiftly glides along the banks of the Blue Juniata, and after awhile he winds his way up the grand old Alleghenies, and again, he is enveloped in total darkness as he passes through the longest tunnel in the world! Fine manufacturing towns and villages are interspersed along the whole route, giving life to the scene. We reached Pittsburg about noon of Monday, took the river road as far as Wellsville, where we changed cars, and arrived in Ravenna shortly after five o'clock P.M.

MANASSAS JUNCTION.

This famous battle-field, of which so much has been said, is nothing more or less than one grand series of inferior earthworks. As the train upon which we were riding halted at this place some two hours, we had an opportunity of visiting several of the fortifications of this rebel stronghold. Compared with our fortifications around Washington, these sink into insignificance. Bull's Run, itself, is the only natural fortification of the place, and we almost wonder at the repulse of our army at this place in July last.

ALEXANDRIA.

This city, situated eight miles below Washington on the opposite bank of the Potomac, with the exceptions of those immense works – Forts Ellsworth and Lyon – presents nothing of note to the eye of the traveler. The spirit of the lamented Ellsworth almost seems to haunt the place.

WASHINGTON.

We arrived in this city early on Saturday morning, and a short walk, after leaving the cars, brought us to Pennsylvania Avenue, the principal street of the city. After obtaining passes and eating a sensible breakfast of ham, eggs, potatoes, bread, butter, coffee, strawberries and cream, currant pie, sponge-cake, and ice-cream, we took a carriage and drove down Pennsylvania Avenue, across to Jersey Avenue, and up Capital Street to the Baltimore Depot, where we arrived just in time to miss the train! We now went up to the Capitol which is a splendid stone ediface situated on a height of ground overlooking the whole city. The House of Representatives and Senate Chambers are grand and costly audience rooms. In the Rotunda are many statues of marble and large costly paintings. The Senate was in session, and its grand old walls rung with the wrangling debates of its many distinguished occupants. The Capitol-grounds with its shady walks, sparkling fountains and flower-beds, affords a pleasant retreat to the traveler as well as the excited Senator. The next place we visited was the Government Printing Establishment, where *five hundred* persons are employed, *two hundred* of whom are ladies. This is a happy, busy scene. [Apparently, Daniel still had some of the printer's ink in his blood from his days as a newspaper employee.]

BALTIMORE.

The great Monumental City of Baltimore was reached at five o'clock Saturday evening, when we walked up Baltimore Street through Monument Square to Calvert Station. In the centre of Monument Square is a splendid marble statue of Washington, standing upon a pedestal of the same, the whole surrounded by a beautiful iron railing. Two magnificent hotels – the Barnum and the Gilmore – front on this Square. Baltimore is a model city.

HARRISBURG.

We arrived in the beautiful city of Harrisburg, situated upon the right bank of the Susquehanna river, at 3:30 Sunday morning, where we remained until the next morning. The Capitol is situated upon a height of ground overlooking the city, and is built of brick. The grounds are neatly laid out and well shaded. The State Arsenal is upon the ground and the whole is surrounded by a high iron fence. The city water-works are a stupendous work, from the reservoir of which can be seen the Lunatic Asylum, Cemetery, and Camp Curtin. Five hundred rebel prisoners arrived at this camp from the Shenandoah Department on Sunday afternoon and drew a large crowd of spectators.

PITTSBURG.

This city is situated at the junction of the Allegheny and Monongahela rivers and is a large manufacturing place. There are many fine and costly residences upon the Allegheny side. Glad we were to leave this black and dirty city.

Respectfully, D. H. W. [1]

When the above letter appeared in the July 2, 1862 edition of the *Democrat*, three small items pertaining to the 7th Ohio also were printed.

FOR THE 7TH. – DANIEL H. WRIGHT of Co. G, 7th Regiment, will leave Ravenna, July 10, to join his regiment. Letters left for him at the Ravenna Book Store will be duly taken to their destination, all other commissions must be declined as the uncertainty of location and transportation forbid baggage.

CAPT. QUAY is improving in health, but is hardly able to resume his duties. He has been under vigorous treatment and with the needed rest is nearly restored. Capt. Quay and Capt. J. G. Willis leave Ravenna on Friday and will take small matter to the 7th if left at the Ravenna Book Store prior to that day.

M. C. HORTON of Co. F, 7th Regiment, has returned to his home in Nelson. Mr. Horton was taken as prisoner at the Strasburg Hospital where he was serving as Steward, in company with a number of others made prisoners at the same time, and released on parole, he was discharged from further service in the U. S. Army at Washington last week. [2]

HOW THE SEVENTH REGIMENT KEPT THE FOURTH –

The following is from the Cleveland Herald, July 9.

A private letter from a member of the Seventh Ohio Regiment, dated in Camp one mile West of Alexandria, July 6th, mentions the manner in which the Regiment kept the "Fourth." The men were all kept within the camp lines, no passes having been issued. At nine o'clock in the morning the regiment was reviewed by Brigadier Gen. Tyler, after which a few appropriate remarks were made by Chaplain Wright. Serg't Bowler of Co. C read the Declaration of Independence and the regiment was marched back to camp.

In the afternoon the "boys" concluded that some fun was necessary to the proper celebration of the Fourth, so they marched up to one of the officers and bore him off to the Sutler's Quarters where he paid ransom in the shape of oranges and cigars. Emboldened by their success, they proceeded to arrest the other officers and subjected them to the necessity of buying their liberty in the same way, the Colonel himself being captured. Finally the whole Brigade proceeded to surround the quarters of Brig. Gen. Tyler, who surrendered unconditionally and ransomed himself by an order for each regiment to march to its Sutler and be treated at the General's expense, costing him probably $150 to $200.

In the evening the boys of the regiment amused themselves by watching the fireworks at Alexandria and Washington, which could be plainly seen from camp. [3]

Camp Near Alexandria, Va.,
Thursday, July 24, 1862.

Editor Democrat:

Having a few leisure moments and thinking perhaps a few items in regard to the doings of the old Seventh might be acceptable, we will give them.

OUR "SITUATION"

The Seventh with the rest of Tyler's brigade, the 5th, 29th, and 66th regiments, is encamped on a fine elevation just back of Fort Ellsworth and about one mile west of Alexandria. The broad Potomac, dotted with its many steamers, brigs, sloops, barges, and schooners, flows gently oceanward, and presents to our view a pleasing contrast to the rugged peaks of the Allegheny and Blue

Ridge mountains, with which for the past year we have been so familiar. Now instead of the little, insignificant seven-by-nine "shelter tents" (which by the way, were never known to shelter us,) we have the large Sibley tent, and can once more "go in when it rains," without getting wet.

OUR FIGHTING IMPLEMENTS.

The Seventh is now equipped with that long-coveted "shooting iron," the Springfield Rifle, a beautiful piece, which is said to be good for five hundred yards. Had we been armed with these at Port Republic, many more of the foul traitors under "Old Stonewall" would have been reported "gone up" (or *down*!) at their next roll-call. We hope to try our new pieces soon.

THE WAR HORSE.

Since the promotion of our much beloved Colonel, W. R. Creighton, the officers and men of the Seventh have presented him with a fine and handsomely equipped horse. The animal is of light chestnut color and quite spirited. The Colonel also has been presented with a beautiful sword and sash by his eager and willing followers. *Vive la* Colonel.

HEALTH OF THE BOYS.

Never was the health of the Regiment better than at present. The hospital is almost empty. When we arrived here from furlough last week, we found your correspondent Davis G. Steen [Stein], suffering from the effects of a severe bayonet wound received by the falling of a comrade in front of him while going out on review at a double-quick. The bayonet entered a little above the abdomen, and running along under the skin came out just under the heart. Truly a narrow escape. He is doing well and is now able to walk out. Frank Eldridge, Chas. L. King, and Marion Hoover of Co. G who were wounded at Port Republic are at Clifburn Hospital, Washington, and doing well. Nothing has, as yet, been heard from our much respected Sergeant, J. R. Loucks, who was wounded and taken prisoner at Port Republic. [Laucks was severely wounded in the right thigh and left on the field at Port Republic. He died from his wounds at Staunton, Virginia on November 1, 1862.[4]]

"THE GREAT WAR PAPER."

We are in daily receipt of the latest news from New York, Philadelphia, Baltimore, and Washington through the enterprise of numerous newsboys. "The great war paper," the Philadelphia Inquirer, which is brought into camp every forenoon on horse-back by the "funny man," who cries: "Here we are with the great war paper; our men surrounding them; hemming them in; driving them," etc., is the favorite paper with us, furnishing accurate and reliable information from all parts of our strong Republic.

GRAND REVIEWS.

Of late, grand reviews have been the order of the day. Yesterday, the Third Brigade, Gen. Tyler, the Fourth Brigade, Gen. Carroll, the 68th Illinois, the 69th New York, and two Regiments of Cavalry were reviewed by Gen. Cook on the large parade grounds back of Fairfax Seminary Hospital, where some months since, Gen. McClellan reviewed 75,000 troops. We had the pleasure of witnessing this review at a respectful distance, which was worth seeing.

OUR OFFICERS' WIVES.

Several of our officers are at present enjoying the society of their inestimable ladies, who seem to really admire the busy scenes of the merry camp. Would that more of our lady friends might visit us to make glad the heart of the "bould sojer boy."

HOW WE AMUSE OURSELVES.

After the drills and reviews of the day are over, and "Old Sol" has retired to his couch, the boys gather together in groups, sing, tell yarns, pitch quoits, exert the muscles with boxing gloves and gymnastics, and some will go down to the river when the tide is out and *enjoy a quiet* hour in fishing. While the wily fish is biting the hook, ten thousand mosquitoes are biting the *amiable* fisherman! Such was our experience an evening or two since.

CAMP RUMORS.

It is rumored in camp this morning that we are under marching orders. Some say to McClellan's lines, and some say we are going with Pope. Time will tell. Will write again should anything of interest "turn up."

     Respectfully,   D. H. W. [5]

Little Washington, Rappahannock Co., Va.,
Monday morning, August 4, 1862.

Mr. Editor: -- Since our last to you, the "fortunes of war" have removed us from the border, and we are again in the heart of rebeldom, where foul treason with all its wicked associations silently lurks. We are encamped upon a fine knoll, a short distance east of Little Washington and about seven miles from Sperryville. Last Friday week, the Third Brigade left Camp Wade near Alexandria and all the enjoyments of camp life near a city, taking the cars by the way of Manassas and Warrenton Junction to Warrenton, where we arrived at ten o'clock on Saturday forenoon. Here we "pitched our moving tents, a day's march nearer" Dixie, and awaited "further orders." Early on Thursday, the last day of July, after four days hard work, our pension-worthy "M. D.'s" [mule drivers] with their long-eared charges appeared upon the ground, and soon after, all of our "company trash" was snugly packed into the different huge army wagons, and we were ready to march, but the stubborn mules "wouldn't budge an inch." What was to be done now? Three stout hardy men from each company in the brig- ade were detailed, with ropes, whips, etc., [and] fifteen miles was worried through, after killing one "M.D." and seriously injuring several others. The next evening, after several hinderances, occasioned by the "backwardness is coming forward" of the mules, we arrived at this place where we are now waiting "further orders." All praise is due to our patient and persevering "M. D.'s."

REVIEW BY GEN. POPE.

Yesterday, the popular and worthy commander of the Army of Virginia, Maj. Gen. Pope, reviewed his troops in the vicinity of Little Washington. At about seven o'clock in the morning, we were marched to a large field, a mile distant, where we were soon drawn up in line of battle five brigades of infantry, six batteries of artillery, and several squadrons of cavalry, which one year ago numbered over 20,000 troops but whose ranks are now somewhat diminished. All was now silent, and a grander or more imposing scene never presented itself to our view. Soon the artillery opened a heavy fire from their guns which reverberated in thunder tones through the surrounding valleys. Again all was still, and after five minutes of silent waiting, a noise is heard upon the extreme right wing, and "Hail to the Chief" is played by the different bands along the whole line, while, on their richly caparisoned chargers, Major Generals Pope and Banks followed by several Brigadier Generals, Aide-de-camps, and their body guard, pass in review down the line. At the sound of the bugle we were drawn up *en masse* in columns of divisions, our rifles stacked, and allowed a few minutes to obtain water and rest. Another blast of the bugle and we all are upon our feet, when in sweet cadence floats the gentle strains of "Old Hundred" upon the clear morning air, after which, while every head is uncovered, prayer ascends to Almighty God in our behalf from the lips of the distinguished officiating clergymen, which is echoed by the thousands of hearts present. After a sermon, (which owing to the low voice of the speaker, we didn't hear and which, of course, did us no good,) the bands played "My Country," "The Star Spangled Banner," "Hail Columbia," and other appropriate pieces. Again the bugle sounds and to lively music we are marched to our several camping grounds and dismissed. Thus ended the grand review of Gen. Pope.

DEPARTURE OF GEN. TYLER.

Last evening after a short and affecting speech to his men, our brave and much beloved and honored General, E. B. Tyler, left us for Washington where he has been sent by Gen. Pope to form a new brigade of the troops now being raised in the North. He is highly esteemed by all who know him as a man of undaunted courage and bravery, and is complemented by Gen. Pope in receiving this new appointment. We understand the appointment is merely a temporary concern and that after organizing the new brigade, Gen. Tyler will return to his brave command, which will in the meantime be commanded by Brig. Gen. Geary.

CHAPLAIN WRIGHT.

Who has a better chaplain than the Ohio Seventh? Echo answers "Who!" It is our candid opinion that there is not another regiment in the field which can boast a more honest, candid, truthful, and beloved chaplain than ours. At the cool hour of twilight yesterday, the Seventh was gathered around the Adjutant's quarters while good old Chaplain Wright prayed for us in an earnest manner and preached to us in his good-natured and happy style, warming the hearts of nearly every one present. He earnestly cautioned us against the sin of lying, stealing, swearing, licentiousness, illustrating the evils thereof in his characteristic manner. He told us of the interest of our friends at home (he having just returned from a visit to Ohio) in our spiritual as well as bodily welfare; told us of the anxious enquiries of fathers, mothers, wives, sisters and brothers, after their absent ones, and that he really came with good greetings from "loved ones at home." After asking Divine blessings upon our heads, the good Chaplain dismissed the service and the crowd dispersed, each and every one feeling that "it was good that he had been there."

SWORD PRESENTATION.

On the arrival of D. C. Wright from home, the boys gathered around to greet him, when he took occasion to present to Lieut. L. R. Davis of Company D a beautiful sword, sash and belt which he said he had been delegated to present to the young Lieutenant in behalf of his friends at home, who had heard of his promotion. The Lieutenant's feelings choked his utterance, and Capt. J. T. Sterling of Co. B was called upon to respond, which he did in a few appropriate remarks. He said in conclusion that he himself was about to leave the old Seventh for a new field of duty, he having been appointed through the kindness of his friends in Ohio to the Lieut. Colonelcy of the 103d Ohio regiment now forming. He spoke with feeling of fifteen months hard service, of our full ranks when we left Ohio, of our fearful decimation, of our courage, and concluded by urging us to greater deeds of valor. The occasion was one of happy moment, Lieut. D was warmly congratulated and the crowd dispersed after giving a hardy "three times three" for the Lieutenant and the same for Capt. Sterling.

OUR BUGLE AND DRUM CORPS.

Since the discharge of our old Silver Cornet Band, we have been "hard up" for music, but this is being made up to us in part by our efficient bugle and drum corps, which is composed of ten buglers and ten drummers detailed from each company in the regiment. This corps will be of great value upon the battle-field as most of the commands can be given by bugle which will be heard, while on account of the ceaseless din and noise of artillery and musketry, it is with difficulty that the voice is heard.

"ON TO RICHMOND"

This is still the cry of our soldiery, and although there are almost insurmountable obsta[cles] in the way, it is the intention, we believe, notwithstanding the threatening attitude of Jeff Davis and his minions, of the federal leaders to take Richmond at all hazards. "Old Stonewall" is down here at Gordonsville with a large force and says he is going up to Washington and Baltimore soon! Wonder if he really contemplates such a thing? He had best be cautious as our Pope has got an eye on him. Foreign interference is "played out" for the present at least, and we soon hope to march into Richmond to the sure and steady music of the "Star Spangled Banner,"

Yours, respectfully,

D. H. W. [6]

Daniel Wright contributed at least fifteen letters to the editor of the *Portage County Democrat*; thirteen of the letters are presented in this work, and two others were written when he was in the three months' service at Camp Dennison and wrote as the "Printer Boy." The letter of August 4th was Cpl. Wright's last correspondence to the editor. His witty, educational, and faithful correspondence ended with his death at the battle of Cedar Mountain on August 9th. Eleven days later, the *Democrat* printed Wright's last letter and his obituary in the same issue. Surely, Daniel Wright's zest for life was deeply missed.

DANIEL H. WRIGHT, JR., DEAD. – This young and valiant soldier was slain at the late battle of Culpepper Court House. He was a resident of Freedom, where his parents now reside – was 23 years of age – an intelligent and upright young man, and faithful to all the trusts reposed in him. He was among the first volunteers more than a year ago, was at Cross Lanes and at the battle of Winchester, and everywhere acquitted himself well and soldierly. – He was one of the Army Correspondents of the Portage County Democrat, and his numerous letters, signed "D.H.W." have been read with great interest. They prove him to have been a young man of great promise, of mind, intelligence and education.

On the first page of to-day's Democrat will be found a letter from his pen. It was written four or five days before his death, and is the last letter of the brave young soldier. It will therefore be read with melancholy interest.

Forever honored and beloved, be our returning brave, who go forth to battle in a cause so holy. [7]

The Battle of Cedar Mountain on August 9, 1862 was the 7th Regiment's severest test. About 12,000 Union troops under Gen. Banks attacked a superior rebel force. Gen. Jackson's Confederate Army numbered about 22,000.

Marching for both sides was treacherous in the hot August weather, thus causing many men to fall out of the columns with heat exhaustion. The opening of the battle involved an extended artillery duel; and when the Union order to advance was given, the 7th Regiment was in front. In this old-fashioned, stand-up fight the Union forces had great success in the beginning, but they finally succumbed to the Confederate counterattack.

Col. Creighton's report listed a total of 37 killed and 153 wounded out of the 370 men of the 7th Ohio who were engaged in the fight.[8]

The following letter is the account of the aftermath of the Battle of Cedar Mountain as told by Pvt. David Stein.

LETTER FROM VIRGINIA.

Camp Seventh Ohio, Near
Culpepper, Va., Aug. 15, 1862.

Ed. Democrat: -- Long before this can reach you, you will have been advised by telegraph of the desperate and bloody contest near this place on the 9th inst., between the "Yankees" under Gen. Pope and the rebels under Gen. Ewell and old "Stonewall." Having been detained in the Hospital at Alexandria, where the regiment left, from the effects of a bayonet wound some time since, I was not in the engagement, therefore can give you no detailed account of the affair, but have heard and seen enough to convince me that Geary's (late Tyler's) Brigade occupied a conspicuous position on the field, and bore the brunt of the battle. I heard just before leaving Alexandria, that our pickets had been driven in and a battle begun, but had no idea that the old Third Brigade would be shoved to the front wing, to the decimated condition of the ranks. But such seems to have been their position, and their loss in killed and wounded shows how desperately they fought to maintain it. Upon reaching this place on Sunday evening (the day after the battle,) I found the town converted into one vast hospital for our wounded. I found most of the Seventh's wounded occupying a large brick church just across the street from the Court House, where they were receiving as much care and attention as could be bestowed upon them here, where no regular hospital had been established. Most of the wounded have been removed to Alexandria and Washington; the wounded officers are all at the former place.

The Seventh went into the fight with 292 men and came out with 191. The officers in the Seventh killed and wounded are Lieut. Johnson, Co. F, killed; Lieut. Brisbane, Co. E, killed; Lieut. Ross, Co.

I, killed; Col. W. R. Creighton, severely wounded – The ball took effect just above the elbow on the left arm, and passing upward lodged in the shoulder blade. Adj. Molyneaux, slightly wounded in the right shoulder; Capt. W. R. Sterling, wounded in the right thigh; Lieut. Reed, severely wounded in left side and leg; Lieut. Hopkins, severly wounded in the face.

The following is the list of casualties in the two Companies from Portage:

COMPANY G,

Killed. – The first name on the list, it becomes my painful duty to record, is that of your able and worthy correspondent and our brave and much beloved comrade-in-arms, Daniel H. Wright. He was one of the color Guards on the day of the battle, and although he had received two severe wounds, his brave and determined spirit would not permit him to leave the field until the fatal ball struck him, and he died, fighting till the last. The others killed in Company G are T. H. Whitmore, H. F. Dindes, Milo Minard, and Henry Howard. The wounded are Orderly Sergeant G. W. Barrett severely in right leg, leg amputated, Sergeant E. M. Lazarus slightly in the knee, Corporal W. F. Callow severely in the shoulder, John H. Douthett severely in arm and side, I. B. Green back of the head and shoulder, Jarvin Holcombe in the side by a piece of shell, Lewis Owen in the side, two ribs broken, S. A. Fuller slightly in the shoulder, Frank Strong severely in the arm and ankle, Wm. S. Gibbons three balls in feet and ankle, S. P. Walker severely in the leg and shoulder, Loren Reed slightly in the hand, G. D. Berthoff slightly in the arm

COMPANY F,

The killed in this Company are Sergeant E. G. Taylor, Hiram Waight, H. C. Case, John Handsom, David Mathews, and S. B. Mathews.

The wounded are Sergeant J. B. Carter slightly, Corporal Benj. Gridley severely, Corporal R. M. Risk severely, P. D. Loomis severely, Thos. Ely slightly, Daniel Jones severely, G. W. Carrin slightly, D. C. Nunemaker slightly, Ezra Brown slightly, leg, Sherman Eatinger severely, Nathaniel Guitchell slightly, Arthur Adams, John Downer lungs, J. F. Oviatt slightly, S. A. Hopkins severely, G. M. Cadwell severely, Ralph Winzenrad severely.

Near the close of the battle as the Seventh (or at least what remained of the Seventh) were going to the rear to which place they had been ordered, they were met by a "red tape" officer who had probably laid back and witnessed the battle at a *respectful distance*, who mistaking the Seventh for the color company of some other Regiment and thinking it an excellent opportunity to "spread" himself, cried out at the top of his voice, "Where are you going with those colors? Take them back or give them to somebody that will not disgrace them." The words were no sooner uttered than two swords were placed in very close proximity to his "bread-basket" and he discovered the inscription on the banner just in time to save his worthless life. "Oh!" said he, "you are the Seventh Ohio, you are the Regiment that has been to the front and were so badly cut up. Excuse me gentlemen, beg ten thousand pardons!" etc., etc. His insignificance protected him, and he was allowed to depart unmolested.

  The Seventh Ohio with the rest of the skeleton brigade is at present encamped near Culpepper. To-day there was a "grand review" of the troops here, and there is some talk of the "higher authorities" of consolidating our whole brigade into one regiment. An operation of this kind would not go down well with the officers and men of the Seventh nor of any of the regiments interested. The Seventh has now been in the service sixteen months, during that time it has been almost constantly on the march and has been in four engagements, each time getting badly cut up, and now when the regiment is scarcely large enough for a Corporal's Guard they would have us throw away our hard earned name; consolidate us with some other regiment and "go in" again immediately. This is what might be termed "riding a free horse to death." But I have no doubt if the Seventh would march and fight till each man has one leg apiece, we would be furnished with *wooden legs* and again ordered to the front while pet Eastern Regiments could lie back and garrison forts, guard little towns, and perform other light duty, "Let em try it onst."

Very respectfully, D. G. S.
Co. A, 7th Ohio. [9]

  No Civil War battle merely ended with the last shot fired. As Pvt. David Stein's previous letter indicated, the battle lingered in the minds of the survivors, and the updated casualty lists added to the sad and bitter memories. Bodies of the dead soldiers of the 7th Ohio were periodically shipped home to Portage County and the *Democrat* printed the sad story of each one. The bloom of the rose of war had withered and only the thorns remained; the unbridled enthusiasm of April 1861 had disappeared. Occasionally, a bittersweet article, such as the following about a released prisoner, would appear in the newspaper.

LETTER FROM MARYLAND.

The writer of the following letter was taken prisoner at Port Republic. The letter has been handed in for publication by his mother, who resides in Streetsborough.

Annapolis, Maryland, Sept. 18, 1862.

Dear Mother: -- It is with pleasure I can inform you that I am once more in the land of liberty, under the stars and stripes – the good old flag that still floats over a part of our once happy country. I am no longer obliged to dodge a rebel bayonet or eat the maggots of Richmond. I left Richmond on the 14th and arrived here on the 16th. All the prisoners held at Richmond, some four or five thousand, were released on parole, myself among the number.

I had much rather have been exchanged and returned to my regiment, but rather than die of starvation or some other horrible death incident to secesh prison life, I gave my word of honor not to take up arms against the "Confederate States" until exchanged.

There are about seven thousand paroled prisoners here. We have a pleasant location, our liberty, and plenty to eat. Each man receives a new suit of clothes. I have not drawn any yet, but will today. We are to paid before long, I understand.

It is rumored the Ohio troops are to be sent to Camp Chase, Columbus. I hope it may be so.

While a prisoner, I spent part of my time in the hospital, but through a kind Providence have been restored to health and I begin to feel like myself again. I wrote you three or four times while a prisoner but do not know as you received any one of my letters. I received one from you bearing date Aug. 23d, in which you stated you had not heard from me since a prisoner. That is the only news I have heard from home since the forepart of May.

You mentioned Serg. Loucks in your letter. The last time I heard from him he was at Port Republic unable to travel. He will come on as soon as he is able. He was badly wounded in the thigh and did not receive the proper treatment. I staid behind to help him off the field and we were both taken prisoners.

Please write immediately,   H. M. H. [10]

[H. M. H. was Cpl. Hiram M. Holton who survived the war. He was mustered out on July 7, 1864. Sgt. James R. Laucks, the friend whom Holton tried to save, died of his wound at Staunton, Virginia on November 1, 1862. [11]]

Although the 7th Ohio was reduced to about 19 % of a full-strength regiment, little time was allowed for to recuperation.. The remnants of the Seventh were destined to participate in the bloodiest, one-day battle of the Civil War, which occurred at Sharpsburg, Maryland on September 17, 1862.

The 7th Regiment was now in Maj. Gen. Joseph K. F. Mansfield's Twelfth Corps and the First Brigade of the Second Division, commanded by Brig. Gen. George S. Greene. The regiment was commanded by Maj. Orrin J. Crane, who would advance to brigade command when Lt. Col. Hector Tyndale was wounded in the fighting.

In Gen. McClellan's piecemeal attack, the Twelfth Corps entered the morning phase of the battle about 7:30 A.M. The Seventh Regiment advanced with Gen. Greene's two brigades over the gently undulating terrain to a plateau opposite the Dunker Church. Amidst the acrid clouds of hovering battle smoke, the yells and screams of the combatants of both sides, the constant booming of artillery and the exploding shells, the crashing of musketry, the heat of the physical exertion and the hot September day, the two brigades made their stand.

For half an hour they held this spot with their ammunition spent and with fixed bayonets. The ammunition was replenished just in time. At 10 A.M. three Confederate regiments dashed out of the woods and crossed the dirt road coming at the Union troops. When the rebels were within seventy yards, Greene's men rose up and delivered a destructive fire. "The enemy fell like grass before the mower, reported Major Crane of the 7th Ohio..." [12]

Almost a month after the Battle of Antietam, Capt. F. A. Seymour of Company G wrote a long letter to the *Democrat* from Louden Heights at Harpers Ferry. Seymour chronicled the events from early August to October 13th.

The main features of the Chattanooga-Ringgold Campaign – The distance from Bridgeport, Ala. to Chattanooga is approximately 30 miles. From Chattanooga to Ringgold, Ga. is about 18 miles. The stars indicate combat locations for the 7th Ohio.

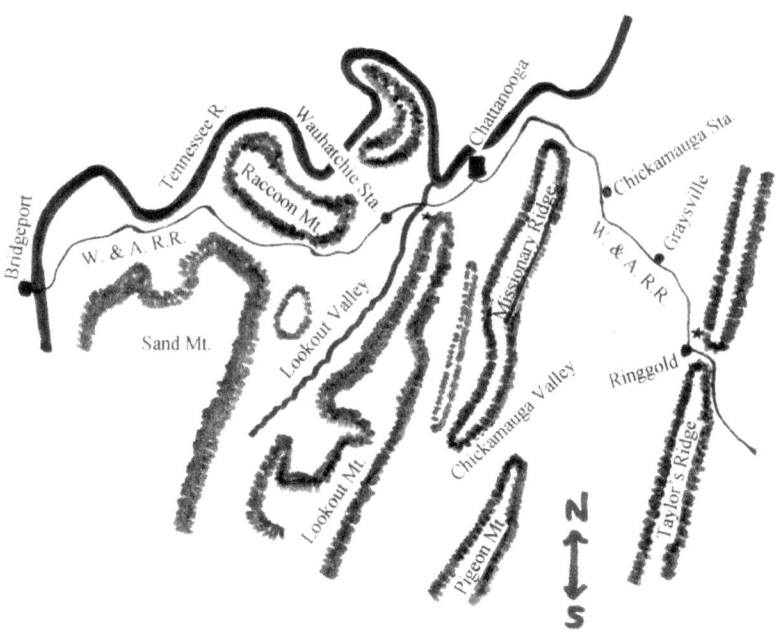

London [sic] Heights, Oct. 13, 1862.

Ed. Democrat: -- Thinking the present whereabouts and recent moves of the 7th Ohio Regiment might be regarded with some degree of interest by your readers, I venture to give you its history since we were put under the command of Gen. Pope. From Alexandria we went to Warrenton, thence to Little Washington, then to Culpepper, with little of interest to the 7th, except the removal of Gen. Tyler from us. At this, the boys at first demurred, but on receiving Gen. Geary, they are better satisfied. From Culpepper the regiment marched to the battle-field on Cedar Mountain, and with the conspicuous part which our regiment bore on that eventful day, you are already familiar.

Here I would be allowed to say one word for the fallen braves of my own little band from Co. G. It is no attempt at flattery or unmeaning eulogy on my part when I say with all sincerity, that a more noble or braver band of men never gave their lives in defence of any cause. Corporal D. H. Wright was a worthy specimen of the Ohio volunteer – respectful and courteous to his superiors, brave and manly in the face of the foe. These qualities won for him the high regard of the officers of his regiment. Minard, Whitmore, Day, Dinges, also acted well their part, and did all their duty with a courage and zeal that others might well imitate, and nobly died in defence of their country's flag; and although lying low in their lonely graves, where neither the booming of the morning gun nor the bugle call to reveille can awake them more, yet they will not be forgotten, for they have left a clear record behind them, which their sorrowing friends have no wish to efface.

The wounded survivors I would not forget. Lieut. S. S. Reed has ever shown himself ready to do all his duty with a prompt and cheerful obedience that entitle him to the respect and gratitude of those whose rights he has gallantly defended. Sergt. George W. Barrett, for whom I shall ever feel the warmest ties of friendship, has proved himself ready for duty, prompt to execute any trust reposed in him. I had learned that upon him I could rely with confidence, and for the terrible loss he has sustained, I trust a grateful people will not be slow to acknowledge his merits and render him needful assistance. [Barrett's right leg was amputated.] It is said that the other survivors of that fatal day are now, or will soon, be ready to join the regiment. Serg't Lazurus, Frank Strong, William Gibbons, S. A. Fuller, S. P. Waller, Gilbert Bertholf, Lewis Owen, are nearly well. God speed their recovery.

After that awful day, our troops fell steadily back to the Rappahannock, and for the most of the time that Gen. Pope was engaged with the enemy [the Battle of Second Manassas], our Brigade, as was the most of Banks' corps, were held in reserves and to no great extent engaged except slight skirmishes, although we were kept under arms all the time and were several times ordered to the front, yet were brought to no general engagement. At last, after marching, countermarching, and using all kinds of strategy to escape, we fell back to the Potomac near Fort Worth. From there, the order came to join the main army and go to Maryland to intercept Jackson, Lee, and Longstreet, who as rumor had it, had invaded Maryland with 300,000 men. [The actual number was closer to 55,000 men.]

On the 4th day of September, our brigade crossed the Potomac from Virginia at Georgetown and moved on the road to Rockville. Our progress was slow and toilsome on of account of the great mass of troops and the enormous supply train necessary to move so large an army.

We made but slow progress but kept moving steadily on to Frederick City.

On the 8th day of September, Col. Asper left the regiment on account of sickness, and acting Major Crane being absent, the command of the regiment devolved upon myself. On the 9th day, Col. Buckley of the 29th Ohio left the brigade, where he had been commanding the last few days, he being no longer able for duty. Lieut. Col. Tindale, of the 28th Pennsylvania Regiment, took command of the brigade which was composed of the following regiments: The 5th Ohio, the 7th Ohio, the 29th Ohio, the 66th Ohio, and the 28th Pennsylvania. [The four Ohio regiments had been so reduced that the 28th Pa. by itself nearly equaled them in numbers.] On the 11th day while halting for a rest, Gen. Cox of our old command came up with his division. He stopped for awhile to see his old friends and was warmly greeted.

We moved on in perfect order; slow of necessity, for we were in three, and some of the time five columns, when on the march, for it would be impracticable for all to pass on one road in a single column. It was a sight magnificent and grand, and from some hilltops we could get a view of our advancing columns stretching far away. We kept steadily on, day by day, until the 13th when we came in sight of Frederick City. As we drew near the town, the sound of artillery broke upon our ears. We were hurried forward with all possible haste; but on coming to the town, found the rebels had fallen back to the mountains and were fortifying to dispute the passage of our advance.

We encamped on the night of the 13th in sight of the town and awaited orders. Soon the order came to be ready to march at the break of day with three days rations. On the morning of the 14th we moved on through town. The people seemed wild with joy to think that the Union troops were to come to their relief. Old ladies, blooming maidens, young girls, little boys with cool pails of water, all striving to be first to do something for the Union soldiers. At nearly every window were displayed the Stars and Stripes by ladies fair, as they bid us welcome and God speed. On through the town we passed, with lighter hearts and footsteps, all feeling that we left friends behind us, and not, as in Virginia, lurking, secret foes to shoot down our pickets.

As we left the friendly city, one might discover the glistening tear in the soldier's eye, as he turned himself around to gaze again, as it brought to mind his home and loved ones.

As we moved on to South Mountain Pass, the booming cannon from the rebel batteries, as they tried to hold our men in check, came thundering through the air. At last, as we came nearer, the heavy roar of infantry told too plainly that a terrible battle was waging. As our artillery was returning the fire from the rebel batteries, Gen. Cox with his division had attacked them and completely flanked them, and before they were aware of his approach, poured a deadly fire upon them, drove them from their stronghold behind stone works with terrible slaughter, leaving their dead piled in heaps, so terrible was their destruction. Gen. Cox and his men won for themselves a name which will not soon be forgotten.

The night of the 14th we encamped at the foot of the mountain in sight of the bloody field. On Monday the 15th, we were early on the march. As we passed up the mountain road, we met a flag of truce borne by a rebel surgeon seeking the body of a Colonel who fell the day before. They lost a General also, and a large number of officers of less rank. It was in this engagement that Gen. Reno fell, a loss severely felt by our men for he was a good man and a brave General.

As we went forward, the road on all sides gave unmistakable evidence of a terrible battle, for on all sides dead men and horses, broken cannon, and all the dreadful carnage of war lay in wild confusion. Not a farm house, or mountain hut, barn or shed, but was filled with the dead and wounded in all forms – some without arms, others with legs cut off by the terrible cannon ball, others too badly wounded to be helped but in their last agonies begging for help.

As we moved on in pursuit of the fleeing foe, our men in good spirits, wrought up by the presence of our great Chieftain, Gen. McClellan, as he rode through the ranks, it was pleasant to see the countenances of our men light up with joy, as they rent the air with cheer after cheer, which was gracefully acknowledged by the gallant General.

After marching till dark this night, the 15th, we bivouaced for the night. On the morning of the 16th we were aroused from our bed on the ground and received the order to march, for our artillery had engaged the enemy on the hill a mile in our front. – Our division was formed under Gen. Green, in quick time were on the move to support the batteries, but after an hour's artillery dueling, the rebels fell back across Antietam Creek. We were formed in close order of division, and the order came to stack arms and make ourselves as comfortable as possible. – Our men set about making coffee, the soldier's only solace, after which, choosing the softest place on the ground, sought that rest and sleep so much needed by our nearly exhausted men, and night setting in, without further orders, we prepared to pass the night; but soon the order came to "fall in" and in a moment we were under arms and on the march which was slow and tedious as all night marches are. We kept on our march until three o'clock in the morning, when arriving at a point near where the rebels were encamped and made a stand, we were ordered to halt and wait the return of the morning. – Our men quickly dropping on the ground were quietly sleeping as if there was nothing to disturb them on the coming morning. But to the tired and weary soldier, from three o'clock till morning passes quickly away, and scarcely had the first tints of daylight broke upon the Eastern horizon, when the roar of the artillery and musketry startled the slumbering soldier, and the order came to "fall in." With aching heads and benumbed limbs, they quickly obeyed the order and were on the march. After moving a mile to where the enemy were engaging our right wing, we were ordered to halt for our men to make coffee. Fires were soon kindled and the most of our men were able to get their coffee – some that were too slow had to do without, for the order came to advance on the enemy. Our men were formed in column of division, the right in front, our brigade under Col. Tindale of the 28th Pennsylvania, our division under Gen. Green, our corps under Gen. Mansfield. In this order we moved on in solid column till we reached a point of the woods where the enemy were in heavy force and were holding our men in check. At this point we deployed our brigade in line of battle to the right, the 7th regiment on the right of the brigade, and marched into the woods where the rebels were masked behind a fence, lying flat on the ground, their dirty gray (not uniforms) but rags, were so near the color of the ground that at first it was difficult to see where they were, but we soon learned, for the leaden hail came thick and fast, and told upon our men for three of Co. G had been already wounded. Our men soon discovered their hiding place and most terribly did they avenge their fallen comrades. After about twenty minutes of terrible fighting, we drove them from their shelter and put them to flight. In pursuing, as we advanced to their hiding place, the dead lay in piles, so sure and deadly had been our fire. – They fell back through a field of standing corn, our men hotly pursuing, literally covering the ground with dead and wounded, capturing hundreds of prisoners of all grades from Colonels down to privates, besides a large number of colors. The carnage of that bloody field was terrible beyond all description. No language can describe, nor pen ever picture it.

After following them a mile or so, giving them no time to rally their confused and disordered ranks, our fire slackened for our ammunition had given out, although each man had from 60 to 70 rounds at the commencement of the fight. So it may safely be inferred that there was some shooting done. An Orderly being dispatched for ammunition by Gen. Green, our men lay down upon the ground, when shot and shell went screaming through the air above us, yet so as not to harm us. After waiting half an hour, the ammunition having been brought up and our cartridge boxes being replenished, we changed our line of battle to the right and marched to a slight elevation of ground towards which the enemy were advancing. As we gained the top of the hill, they were advancing upon us in columns of regiments. – On they came with steady tramp determined to gain what they had lost the last two hours. Our men, nothing daunted, thought to show them a specimen of the Yankee – accordingly ordered our right to advance as skirmishers which they did with orders to fall back at a given signal. Our regiment suddenly falling back under a hill, lay down, calmly waited their approach. On they came confidently expecting to overwhelm us with their superior force as to numbers. Our skirmishers falling back to where the regiment lay, drew them on, until within about fifty yards of our lines; then, suddenly rising to our feet, we poured so deadly a fire upon them, that they were completely broken and confused, our men following them with volley after volley with such terrible effect that they again retired in confusion and almost total rout. They took shelter again in a piece of heavy standing timber half a mile or more back, to where our troops pursued with victorious shouts, capturing prisoners without number, and still driving them from their shelter; our right acting as skirmishers in the woods, driving them from tree to tree, and held the ground we had gained for an hour or more, they holding their men as best they could and fighting with the desperation of fiends, seemed determined to perish rather than yield. The ground from the hill, from which we had driven them in wild disorder back to the woods, was all the way strewed thick with the wounded and slain, and presented a spectacle of horror at which the heart saddens and grows sick in beholding.

The dead lying mangled and torn in all the horrid ghastliness of death was a sight terrible beyond all conception. The wounded Rebel and Union soldiers lay side by side, apparently forgetting they ever were enemies, piteously asking for water and help from those who, a short half hour ago, were seeking each other's life with all the intensity of hatred which man is capable. A rebel officer, upon being offered water, looked up with his eyes full of tears – said he did not expect that, but supposed he would be bayoneted.

It was on this part of the field that our loss was the heaviest. It was here that Corporal Lazurus of Co. G and Sergt. Carter of Co. F fell, in the thickest of the fight; and I may be allowed to say that two better soldiers never fell on any battlefield. And terrible and heart crushing as it is to friends, they have the mournful satisfaction of knowing that they died at their post, in the midst of the dangers from which they never for a moment shrank or faltered. They nobly died with their face to the foe.

Gen. Green ordered us back to rest our men, as our brigade commander, Col. Tindale had been severely wounded, and as our troops had been constantly under fire of the hottest kind since six in the morning. It was after one P.M. and our men were glad to get a chance to rest for they were nearly exhausted. The day was very warm and the work terrible. Before falling back, both Col. Tindale and Gen. Green paid us a high compliment for our good order, coolness and courage in battle. He said he was proud of his Ohio troops – they were worthy of any commander. It was with much sorrow that we learned at this time of the fall of our Corps commander, Gen. Mansfield. We had learned to admire him and believed him a good man as well as a good general.

Gen. McClellan was everywhere on all parts of the field, giving orders and encouraging his troops. You could tell on what part of the field the general was passing by the deafening cheers that rent the air. [This is fanciful thinking on the part of Seymour or hearsay because McClellan commanded from a distance at his headquarters at the Pry House.] It will be seen that the work he had to do was of a magnitude which most minds would have been inadequate to perform.

(The writer here gives a detailed account of Burnsides' terrible struggle with the enemy, when it was impossible to furnish him adequate reinforcements, and proceeds.) [This note was inserted by the editor of the *Democrat*.]

As the darkness set in, our little shattered brigade was ordered again to the front. Being in command of our regiment, on receipt of the order I soon had the 7th under arms, and we were on the march. Arriving within 80 rods of the enemy's lines, we were ordered to halt and wait for orders. Giving our tired men the order to rest, they were soon lying on the ground, each with his musket firmly grasped, ready for that oft repeated word, "fall in." Receiving no further orders for the night, our men were soon in sleep, forgetful of the events of that never to be forgotten day. Nearly all night the pickets kept up their dueling and many a soldier that night went out to duty who returned no more.

On the morning of the 18th, I begged permission to go back to the field in order to obtain the remains of Corp. Lazurus and Sergt. Carter, and receiving an order from Gen. Green to take as many men as I needed to bury the dead from our regiment, I obeyed the order, taking with me some twenty men with and stretchers and [illegible], we started on our sorrowful mission to perform the last rites to our fallen comrades. On arriving at the point where our men had fallen, we collected all we knew to have been killed, took them to a burying ground neatly enclosed, and there in their soldier's grave, put up a head board to their graves, dropped a tear over their ashes, and bid them farewell.

All agree it was the most terrible fight that ever occurred on American soil. As we moved on, on all sides for two or three miles the ground was still covered with the unburied dead, the rebels having stole away in the night leaving their dead for us to bury. The Provost

Marshal has reported five thousand dead rebels which he has buried and not through then. It is said, and not with exaggeration, that their loss after leaving Manassas was sixty thousand men. This is their own account, and forty thousand crossed to Maryland that never went back. A terrible retribution after their pompous boast that they would desolate Pennsylvania. [The actual Confederate loss at Antietam was about 10,700; the Union loss was about 12,410. [13]]

As we marched on through Sharpsburg, it looked as if some terrible earthquake had visited it, so torn and shattered was it with shot and shell.

(The writer gives an account of his occupancy of Maryland Heights with the 7th Regiment, which the great length of his communication obliges us to omit.) [The editor's note.]

On the 2d of October Gen. Geary resumed command, having left us wounded at Cedar Mountain. The boys were glad to see him.

We turned out to see President Lincoln as he came to review us. Our brigade turned out, what remains of us, and gave him a warm reception. He looks hale and hardy, not care worn, as might be expected from the pressure of business that throngs him.

We have skirmishing every day, more or less. As we came through Harper's Ferry, our boys were all anxious to see the old Engine House where John Brown held Virginia chivalry so long at bay. The old port holes pierced for guns have been plastered up but plainly show where they were.

It is said that Government will immediately rebuild the public works at Harper's Ferry and resume the manufacture of arms, and that troops are to be kept here this winter. It is hoped it may be the lot of the 7th Regiment to remain here – to stay at least long enough to fill up our thinned ranks.

F. A. SEYMOUR,
Capt. Co. G, 7th Regt., O.V.I.

P. S. – Please say, in answer to numerous inquiries by letter, which with the business of the regiment on my hands I can find no time to answer, that the wounded are well cared for – and are at present at Frederick City. It would not be best for friends to visit them – thinking to get them home; for in no case will the Medical Board allow it. They will, as soon as they can be moved with safety, be sent North. Alson Coe has died since the battle. He died the 21st – the rest are doing well. [14]

The Bully Seventh

A correspondent of the New York Times, writing from the army says:

The famous Seventh Ohio is also encamped on Loudon summits. The "bully Seventh," as it is familiarly termed, has been reduced to a mere skeleton of a regiment, (numbering less then one hundred men,) not by sickness or desertion, but by bloody work at Cross Lanes, Winchester, Port Republic, Cedar Mountain, and Antietam. Company C, originally one hundred strong, made up of college boys, mostly acquaintances of your correspondent, have but one officer, and he a non-commissioned one left. At Cross Lanes the Captain and Lieutenants were lost, and in succeeding engagements it was so decimated as to be able to muster but twenty-one at the battle of Cedar Mountain. Seventeen of these were killed and wounded in that engagement. E. B. Atwater of this company, while the battle was progressing at Sharpsburg, fearlessly sprang forward in front of his regiment and captured the Colonel of the 11th Mississippi, S. F. Butler. Not liking the idea of being run through with a bayonet, he surrendered himself to the *mudsill* private. Remarking, "I am your prisoner," and delivering into his hands a splendid belt and sword which the brave fellow now has. [15]

Letter From Washington.

Washington City, D. C.,
Oct. 19, 1862.

Ed. Dem.: -- Perhaps a few lines from this quarter may not be uninteresting to your readers. The city is now comparatively quiet; but new regiments and recruits for the old ones continue to arrive daily, *en route* for the field. The recruits for the 7th which arrived here some time since, have been sent on to the regiment. They were a fine set of looking men and seemed anxious to be "armed and equipped" and have a chance at the "rebs." I think they have got into a favorable regiment to have their wishes granted in that respect. But by the time they have followed the banner of the "Seventh" for ten months or a year, they will quite likely think of the days when they were "better off," or sigh for "a lodge in some vast wilderness," or exclaim in the language of the poet, "Johny, why did you go for a soger."

The Capitol building, which a few days ago was filled with wounded soldiers from McClellan's late battle fields, is now nearly cleared, the wounded having gone to Northern cities.

The Seventh Ohio is at present encamped on Loudon Heights near Harper's Ferry, where they will probably remain long enough to drill the new recruits and reorganize the regiment. A few days ago I had the pleasure of meeting N. D. Clark, Esq., of your town, the first Ravennian I have come across in a longtime. Gen. E. B. Tyler was also in the city a few days since, but has returned to the front. The General is making an effort to get back the old Third and attach it to his new brigade. This is a move in the right direction and one that, should it be successful, would meet the hardy approval and mutual good feeling of all concerned. – Tyler while in command of the old Third, by his firm and truly military discipline, his prompt attention to the wants and comforts of the men, his courteous bearing towards all, and his cool courage and good generalship on the battlefield, had won not only the respect, but the confidence and warm attachment of all, and it was with the deepest regret that we parted with him in July last, when he was appointed by Gen. Pope to form a new brigade. The "Old Third" want Tyler again for their commander. Can they have him? He was promised that as soon as he had the new brigade ready for the field he could have the old one back. Will they keep their word?

Very respectfully,
D. G. S., Co. A 7th Ohio [16]

[In this work this is David Stein's ninth and last letter to the editor of the *Democrat*. His accidental bayonet wound evidently kept him from active service. The 23 year old soldier was discharged by the War Department on April 28, 1863.]

An October 22 news article in the *Democrat* quoted a visitor to the Antietam battlefield.

> "…I have a thousand things to tell you of what I saw, but one little item will, I know, peculiarly interest you. In a little grave yard where the children of peace have for years been buried, almost in the very heart of the splendid battle

field of Antietam (which grand fields affords one of the most magnificent landscapes you ever beheld,) I discovered a dozen new made graves. At the head of four were these inscriptions written upon strips of cracker boxes – the improvised tomb boards of our gallant dead:

  Heman Bascom [Pvt. Henry Bacon] killed in battle, September 17th, 1862, Co. H 7th Ohio Vol.
  J. B. Carter, Co. F, 7th Ohio Vol.
  M. Lazurus, Co. G, 7th Ohio Vol.
  Elbridge F. Meacham, Co. B, 7th Ohio Vol.

  I knew by this that your Seventh was there, and in the very heat and front of the battle these "noble fighting fell" [17]

In the aftermath of the Battle of Antietam, the scenes of slaughter still haunted one's conscious memory, and the horror that was endured revisited one in his dreams at night. A soldier writing under the name of "Julius" sat in the camp of the 7th Ohio at Harper's Ferry and penned a lengthy letter to the *Western Reserve Chronicle* in Trumbull County. The excellent letter repeated much of the information previously mentioned by Capt. Seymour in regard to the battle. However, the scenes that haunted "Julius," who fought near the Dunker Church and afterward apparently toured much of the battlefield, cut through the usual patriotic and heroic descriptions of a battle and provided sheer realism. The letter also indicated the resilience of the soldiers, who after such an ordeal at Antietam, were "on the gain."

  In the first charge we captured a twelve pounder rifled gun, made at the "Tredegar works, Richmond," and three stands of colors. As we passed the fence, the dead and wounded lay in an indiscriminate pile and in numbers difficult to imagine.
  The blood lay in pools or ran in crimson streams. To clear the bodies I had to stand upon the top of the fence and jump as far as I could. All over the field the dead lay in long rows, plainly showing the position of every line of battle. Some idea may be gained of the immense slaughter by the fact that on an area of only 700 square feet, with a front of 60,

> *fifty-seven dead bodies lay besides the proportionate number of wounded.* This was immediately in front of our regiment in the first engagement, and at the fence, and were counted the next morning by myself and many others. The slaughter was terrible in the extreme...
>
> I need not describe the scenes of the next two days – They are too horrible. I shall always remember the upturned, disfigured and blackened faces everywhere to be seen upon the field, along the road through the village of Sharpsburg, out to the bridge taken by Gen. Burnside, and the thousand other scenes...
>
> As a regiment, we are "on the gain," although of late there has been considerable illness in camp, owing probably to the water, which is rather deleterious, and the excessive fatigue endured to obtain it, having to go down the mountain fully half a mile. It is hoped that we will soon move our camp to a more favorable locality. We have lately received 190 recruits, some of whom have not been assigned to companies. A number of our boys wounded at Cedar Mountain, returned last evening, having recovered, John Lentz and Joseph Kincaid of our company were among the number, looking and feeling well... [18]

Julius' two comrades were among the fortunate ones. For others, the anguish caused by the battles in 1862 simply did not end when the fighting stopped. One such case was that of David Gridley, an "industrious mechanic" from Franklin Mills who had three sons. Benjamin, the youngest son, had enlisted with the original Franklin Rifles in the first call for volunteers in April 1861.

> "...In the battle of Winchester, Benjamin boldly faced the enemy, and rushed on to victory. In the heat of the contest he received a flesh wound in the leg, that disabled him. He was confined in the hospital thirty days – all that time he was cheerful, and anxious to return to his regiment. As soon as he was able, he came home and staid a few weeks. Full of patriotism, he returned to Virginia, found his regiment the day after the battle of Port Republic. Although he missed that battle, he was a brave soldier. At the Cedar Mountain

Battle, Aug. 9, 1862, he was in the midst of the fight. – There he received a wound that broke his leg above the knee. He was taken to the hospital at Culpepper Court House. On the 20th of August that place fell into the hands of the rebels. His brother William was with him, and permitted to stay and administer to his comfort as best he could. He suffered very much, but bore it with the fortitude of a brave soldier. Death put an end to his suffering October 20th, at the age of 20. – just budding into manhood. His brother saw him laid in a soldier's grave. He [William] was then marched off to Richmond, where our soldiers receive ill treatment and short rations from the hands of the secesh …" [19]

Although William Gridley, Jr. witnessed the death of his younger brother and consequently the filth and miserable rations at Libby Prison in Richmond, Virginia, life began to be a little brighter for him in early November.

>Camp of Paroled Prisoners,
>Near Annapolis, Md.
>Nov. 5th, 1862.

Dear Father: I could not write as much as I wished in my last, and now proceed to give you further particulars as I promised. I have no reason to complain of my treatment while in the South, until I went to Richmond. Benjamin [his deceased brother who died of his wounds at Culpepper Court House] received as much, and even more attention, than the sick and wounded confeds. The ladies of Culpepper, in particular, were very kind, with few exceptions. The nurses in the hospitals were ever ready to give me all the assistance in their power. At Richmond, however, the thing is different. The Home Guards, who have charge of the prisoners are a tyrannical set, and like nothing better than to show their authority over prisoners in their power, while the soldiers in the field, who know what service is, have respect for the soldier, whether friend or foe.

I left Culpepper Wednesday the 22nd of Oct., and arrived in Richmond the next day, Thursday, and was marched immediately to the Libby prison, where they had Pope's officers confined. This was a little the roughest place I ever was in. Dirt on the floor was about two inches deep, and you could see "Confederates" crawling about on the floor and seats, half an inch long. Our food was half a pound of bread, and about six inches of bull beef, (about half cooked,) per day. – I staid in Richmond just a week, but the time seemed like six months.

    We had a pleasant trip to Baltimore, where we arrived Saturday morning, and staid till Monday morning, when we were sent to this place, and turned loose in a field, without tents or blankets, and not even a camp kettle to cook our grub in, or a tin cup to drink our coffee from, without any regulations except a strong guard to keep us in. We are expecting to be sent to Camp Chase every day, but this is only rumor, and we may be obliged to stay here until exchanged. You need not look for me home this winter. I am in hopes I will be exchanged soon.

        Please write me soon.
        Yours as ever,
            Wm. Gridley, Jr. [20]

Chapter Five

"The spring of 1863 beholds us in belligerent attitude"

From December 11-13, 1862 the 7th Ohio Infantry was spared the bloody and humiliating Union defeat at Fredericksburg, where 12,600 northern soldiers fell before the well-entrenched Confederate forces of Robert E. lee. The rebels lost 5,300 men in the battle.[1]

On December 10th the 7th Ohio left Bolivar Heights, crossing the Shenandoah River on a pontoon bridge. By the 15th they had slogged over the soft and soggy terrain to within sight of the lower Potomac. They encamped after crossing Naabso Creek. The march continued past Dumphries, but then the regiment returned to Dumfries and set up camp with the 5th Ohio and 66th New York.[2]

On December 26th, elements of the Confederate Cavalry under Jeb Stuart made five charges against the three infantry regiments at Dumphries. It was a stand-up fight for the 7th Ohio which fought in line and without entrenchments. The rebel troopers failed to crack the Union line. Stuart concluded that he could not budge the determined infantry and he withdrew. In the engagement the 7th Ohio lost one killed, 8 wounded, and 14 taken prisoner.[3] The lone death in the 7th Ohio was that of Private Austin Bull, one of the original Tyler Guards.

> Death Of Another Soldier – At the late skirmish at Dumfries, Va., in the rebel Stuart's raid, **Austin Bull**, of Co. G, 7th Regiment O.V., was killed. He was of the first to enlist in Company G and has been in the service since the beginning. He was a son of **Samuel Bull** of Brimfield. His age was 28 years …

After giving the above report, the *Portage County Democrat* then printed the Surgeon's consoling, yet somewhat gruesome, letter to the dead soldier's parents.

DUMFRIES, Dec. 29th, 1862.

To the Parents of Austin Bull:

DEAR FRIENDS: -- The papers have undoubtedly brought you the unhappy news of which my letter is to be only a more particular account. Last Saturday our forces were engaged by the enemy, and among the mortally wounded was your son. I saw him a short time after his wound. A cannon shot struck him across the thighs about three-fourths the way up from the knees, carrying away the front of his limbs, and the bone in one of them. The large arteries were torn off, and he bled to death. I told him he could not live long, though he might for an hour or two. He wished to die immediately, his wound was so painful; but he bore it bravely. He desired me to write you and tell you of his death, and that he died a faithful soldier.

I asked him if he knew what it was to be a Christian. He said he did. He was a Christian once, but had fallen away. I tried to convince him of the fullness of Christ if he was only penitent and had faith. He knew what it was. Christ could go with him through the dark valley. He prayed, so inarticulate, it was impossible to recognize his words. About this time our lines fell back , and I was obliged to leave him, as we had no means of carrying him off the field. He requested to be left there. I doubt not with his Christian education he was enabled to find Christ precious to his soul, and that he died happy. Yesterday morning he was brought in from the field, and during the course of the day buried in a box near the old Court House, just East of some evergreen bushes. A head board marks his resting place, plainly marked.

I do not know that I can offer words of comfort. Be assured we all sympathise with you in his loss. I have been with the Regiment too recently to have much acquaintance with him.

Very respectfully, &c.,
E. HITCHCOCK,
Asst. Surg., 7th Reg. O.V.I. [4]

The remains of Pvt. Bull were shipped home in early February, 1863. "... Mr. John Rhodenbaugh, of Franklin, went on at the instance of the family to procure the remains, and by his perseverance, in the midst of many difficulties, finally overcame all obstacles, and succeeded in his mission." [5]

Because the regimental officers of all units were expected to lead their men into battle and to position themselves in the front of the fighting, attrition in the leadership roles was often a problem. In February, Capt. Seymour Reed of the old Tyler Guards was forced by the nature of his wound to resign.

> Capt. S. S. Reed. Of Co. B, 7th Regiment, has resigned his command and returned home to his residence in Rootstown. His resignation was caused by physical disability, caused by the wound received at the battle of Culpepper. It will be remembered he was wounded in the leg, and he fails to recover the use of his limb so as to endure heavy marches, and hence he voluntarily relinquishes a command which he could not effectively sustain. Capt. Reed leaves the service with the high respect of his company and Regiment. – He has been a faithful and capable officer. He left the Regiment at Dumfries. [6]

On March 15th, Lt. Col. F. J. Asper announced his resignation in a lengthy letter to the *Western Reserve Chronicle*. Being physically unable to continue his military endeavors, Asper intended to return home and to pursue "the peaceful calling of the law." Asper's disability was "occasioned by an inflammation of the sinovial membrane of the joint of the right knee, brought by a strain because of the weakness of the leg from the wound received March 23, 1862 at the battle of Winchester." The surgeon expected Asper to receive at least half a pension. It was difficult for Asper to say good-bye to the men of his command.

> …During last week I visited the regiment to say farewell, and cheer the men by such words as I could speak to them. It was very sad for me to this. Some of them stepped forward with me on the week after the assault on Fort Sumter, had volunteered with me for three years at Camp Dennison, had been brave and true soldiers and companions in arms, had endured with me many a hardship and disaster in battle, had when bullets flew thick and fast and when pressed by overwhelming numbers, stood firm at my bidding and retrieved the fortunes of the day at Winchester, when the Brigade and a portion of the regiment for a time was in confusion; they are the heroes, every one, of many a hard fought battle; they have been under my command, treating me with the highest re-

spect, obeying every order cheerfully and with soldier-like promptness, -- and when I came to sat farewell and be separated from them, and not permitted longer to share their honor and glory, it was indeed a sad and trying hour to me...[7]

Also in mid-March, a member of the old leadership of the 7th Ohio was having temporary problems with the military authorities. The *Portage County Democrat*'s editor could not hide his chagrin at the close of the following article.

> **Gen. E. B. Tyler Under Arrest**. – No little surprise was produced in this community, the home of Gen. Tyler, last week, by the announcement that he had been pit under arrest. A correspondent of the Cleveland *Herald*, writing from Falmouth, Va., Feb. 27th, ascribed the arrest to the personal jealousy of Gen. Humphreys of Pennsylnania. The writer of the letter says:
>> No reason was assigned for this strange procedure, nor can a valid one, with any tolerable degree of certainty, be surmised. Yesterday passed away without any clearing up of the mystery, or any explanation in regard to the matter.
>
> It is reported here in Ravenna, that the arrest was caused by the alleged offense of having overstayed his leave of absence. His friends here believe that the arrest is merely technical, and that he will soon be all right again, and are awaiting further developments with interest.
> What was particularly annoying was that the arrest was made just at the time when the splendid horse and equipments heretofore spoken of were to have been presented, and that ceremony was prevented.[8]

Meanwhile, the new leadership of the 7th Ohio expressed itself in a strongly patriotic letter to the *Chronicle* which gave the letter the following introduction: "The Loyal Voice of the Fighting Ohio Seventh, and the Brave Men who stand Shoulder to Shoulder With Them." The officers were highly incensed by the Copperhead movement back home in Ohio and of the political stance of that state's Clement Vallandigham. The letter was sent from the headquarters of the 7th Ohio at Dumfries, Virginia; and it was signed by the Seventh's Col. William R. Creighton who was commanding the brigade, Maj. Orrin J. Crane of the 7th Ohio, Lt. Col. Powell of the 66th Ohio, and Lt. Col. Clark of the 29th Ohio. These men wanted nothing less than total victory.

...The spring of 1863 beholds us in belligerent attitude, ready at the most favorable opportunity, to strike again for "our Union, our Constitution, and the maintenance of our laws." Month after month the Ohio soldier has been in the field, and his comrades one after the other, have testified by their deaths their devotion to their country; while the great people at home have divided themselves into two parties, each claiming to have the same end in view, but diverse means of attaining that end; the one by upholding and sustaining the Government, in a determination to fight the contest out; the other by opposing the Administration and calling for compromise.

The latter class are traitors; enemies in the dark; more to be feared than the armed rebel before us; and we would respectfully call them to *Attention!* ...

We cannot, dare not, must not compromise. Compromise with *treason*?

It would be a "compromise with iniquity, a compound of heaven and hell." The coming generation would curse us, and our name would be a by-word of obloquy among the nations. While one traitor lives, we will oppose him. No compromise! No, peace! ...

The above article has been published to the Ohio Regiments at this post, and they unanimously endorse the sentiments therein contained. [9]

While the 7th Ohio was waiting and preparing for the "favorable opportunity" to strike again for the Union, Gen. Joseph Hooker replaced Gen. Ambrose Burnside at the helm of the Army of the Potomac. "Fighting Joe" cut the bureaucratic red tape, and rations and other supplies flowed to the needy fighting men. Mail service received Hooker's attention, and communication between the "boys" and their friends and loved ones at home alleviated the worry and "the blues." Many lucky soldiers were granted furloughs on a rotation basis. More attention was paid to drilling which not only sharpened discipline, but also prevented idle hands and minds doing the Devil's work. Morale was vastly improved over those dark, cold, wintry days that followed the Battle of Fredericksburg. Soon, the bombastic Gen. Hooker was exclaiming about this being the finest army on the face of the planet and what he was going to do to "Bobby Lee."

While Hooker was jockeying the Army of the Potomac into position to attack Lee, the common soldier was more concerned with his own immediate welfare than he was with grand strategy. Private John W. Dawes of Company D , 7th O.V.I., was one such soldier. From April 18-22, Pvt. Dawes wrote of matters that were important to him: staying warm and dry, marches to who knows what or where, and the sights and people that he saw. He sent his lengthy account to the *Warren Constitution*.

The *Constitution* was a Democratic newspaper. Its political position was stated in an editorial that appeared adjacent to the printing of Dawes' letter.

> …We have repeatedly stated that the abolition party was for a dissolution of the Union, and carried on war for that purpose … Come go with the Democracy. We are for the Union as it was – we are against dividing or splitting it so that it cannot be got together again. We are for maintaining the Constitution as our fathers made it. We are in favor of law and order and against usurpation and corruption. [10]

It is noteworthy that Pvt. Dawes' account appeared in the *Constitution* as a nonpolitical letter, although he did endorse Lincoln's actions regarding the bombardment of Charleston. The following are extracts of Pvt. Dawes observations.

Dumfries, Va., April 18, 1863.

Dear friends at Home:

…From the date of "striking tents" until the 17th, we labored hard, and almost incessantly, in erecting barracks; but at that date we received orders to prepare for a march, which caused momentary disaffection among our troops and put a quietus to any other preparations for comfortable quarters. Dissatisfied, not because we wish to remain idle throughout the season, but because we had labored exceedingly hard during the week, and taken such pains in constructing new quarters, which we expected to occupy for a few weeks at least, but we are permitted to occupy them for a few nights only. [These were the usual structures of logs and boards, roofs made of shelter tents, and large enough for 4-6 persons.]

Yesterday's couriers from the front, however, state that the infantry remain at Falmouth and Fredericksburg; but a large cavelry [sic] force under General Stoneman had gone out and engaged the enemy's cavelry at Culpepper. The same also states that Stoneman's forces were successful; that the enemy met with a severe loss in killed, wounded, and prisoners; of which it is rumored, we have taken upwards of 600 – supplies have been ordered here for the benefit of the prisoners, who are to pass through to morrow en route north. The 6th Ohio cavelry [many of whom were from Dawes' home area] suffered great loss in the above engagement; their killed and wounded numbering forty. The intelligence of the failure of the bombardment at Charleston [S.C.] had a tendency to dispirit our troops *pro tempore*; but today they are pleased to hear that President Lincoln is dissatisfied with the affair, and notifies diplomatic circles that it will not answer, after six months preparation, to fire a few guns and thus abandon such an undertaking. His language is plain, every word replete with meaning, and in substance the attack must be renewed, and not given up so long as there shall be an iron-clad left.

Sunday, April 19th.

We "strike tents" to morrow morning after "reville." Every soldier is required to carry seven days rations, in addition to his knapsack of clothing, fire-arms, &c. The first R. I. Cavalry are now here to relieve us. Their "band," which is mounted, is discoursing sweet music to-day.

Acquia Landing, April 22nd, 1863.

In compliance with orders, previously issued on the morning of the 20th we "slung knapsacks" and commenced the march leading in the direction of Stafford court house ... It rained very nearly all day, and quite all night. It was warm, and from free prespiration [sic] and the rain, the soldiers were completely drenched. Deep mud, consequently bad roads ... Resumed our march at 7 A.M. and went into camp at 1 P.M. at a point two miles west of Acquia landing. It was a fine day for marching, and the soldiers in apparently fine spirits. Stopped at a farm house on the way, and met with an old lady one hundred and seven years of age. She was manufacturing rolls with hand cards. Being interrogated the length of the time she had lived there, replied, "don't know sir, right smart of years." She appeared hearty, but "non compos mentis."

There is to be a "grand review" to morrow, which is precursory of a movement forward...[11]

[John W. Dawes was 29 years old when he mustered for three years on August 15, 1862. By order of the War Department he was transferred to Co. B of the 5th Ohio on October 31, 1864 after he re-enlisted. The 5th O.V.I. listed Dawes as being 38 years old. He mustered out at McDougal General Hospital, New York Harbor, on May 26, 1865.]

On April 30th, the 7th Ohio crossed the Rappahannock River and arrived at Chancellorsville at 2:00 P.M. Their corps, the 12th, stretched from the now famous Chancellorsville House to a church 1½ miles away. The men immediately began to cut down the brush and scrub pines of this almost impenetrable thicket and to construct abatis.

Early the next day, Friday, May 1st, the Union Army advanced to a commanding ridge at the edge of this hell of scrub pine and brush which was called the Wilderness. The 7th Ohio was in the second line of battle. At this critical moment, General Hooker lost faith in his original battle plan and perhaps in his own ability to command an offensive. He decided to withdraw and to go on the defensive.

In the late afternoon, the 7th Ohio was ordered back, and the men took a position directly south of the brick house. Just before dark, the rebels attacked Knapp's Battery on their left, and the 7th Ohio was ordered to support the battery. By the time the regiment arrived, the attack had been repelled.

The Seventh supported Knapp's Battery that night and until noon of the following day, May 2nd when they were ordered forward to support the skirmishers. That night, they returned to their original position near the Chancellorsville House.

Late in the afternoon of May 2nd, the Seventh Ohio heard tremendous firing to the right of the Union line. It was Stonewall Jackson's Corps rolling up the Union's 11th Corps on the right flank. Later in the darkness, Jackson was severely wounded by his own men, and Jeb Stuart assumed command of the Confederate left. On May 3rd, the Confederates continued to press the Union right flank toward the Chancellorsville crossroads, The 7th Ohio fought with the enemy in their sector all day, often under severe shelling and musketry. They were intensely enraged when their own artillery killed one soldier and wounded several others in the 7th Ohio.

The Seventh was moved toward U. S. Ford where they occupied a rifle pit a half mile from the Rappahannock River. On May 5th, they were relieved by the 5th Ohio. The Seventh then moved further to the left and were deployed in the trenches. The rest of the Union Army was retreating back across the Rappahannock.

Early on May 6th, the Seventh crossed the river on a pontoon bridge. Varying casualty reports have been given for the 7th Ohio's participation at Chancellorsville. Lawrence Wilson, the Regiment's historian, reported 16 killed, 62 wounded, 21 missing for a total of 99.

By May 7th, the 7th Ohio was back at Acquia Creek. The mood of the majority of the soldiers was one of anger, not of disconsolation. They had marched well, fought well, and suffered much, only to be out-generaled again. Major Wood in his 1865 regimental history of the Seventh remarked, "The immediate battle was not a defeat; at least it has not been considered as such ... The retreat alone turned a prospective victory into a humiliating defeat... It can be said by way of apology only, that while at Chancellorsville the army maintained its reputation for bravery and endurance, the enemy manifestly looked upon it as a fruitless victory." [12]

A day after returning to Acquia Creek, a young private in Company A penned a letter to a friend in Cleveland. His letter found its way into the *Cleveland Morning Leader* just one week later.

Camp Near Acquia Creek,
May 8th, 1863.

Friend –: I was glad to hear from you once more. I would have written to you sooner, had I a chance. I have had no rest since the twenty-seventh of last month. I suppose you have already heard of the fight across the Rappahannock. Our regiment was under fire of artillery for three days. Charles H. Cheney, of our company, (A) was killed on the first of May; he was killed by our Battery. We also had two men wounded at the same time, and way. On the second of May, we were supporting a battery of rifled cannon, the enemy opened on us twice that day, and got the worst of it every time. The last time they had two caissons blown up, in the short space of fifteen minutes, and some prisoners said that the six guns were dismounted in the same way. Our regiment opened the ball by driving in the enemy's skirmishers and reconnoitering the enemy's position.

We lost this time our Color Bearer, John G. Craig, of our company. While we were falling back the enemy commenced shelling us again; firing commenced on our right, where the eleventh corps were. Such cannonading I never heard before. The eleventh corps were taken by surprise, they broke in every direction; we halted some of them and tried to turn them back, but it was no go. Here is what one of them said, when we halted him! "Where are you going?" "My regiment is all cut up, and my gun won't go off; it has been loaded for six weeks." Lieutenant How then said: "an't you ashamed of yourself, running away?" He replied, "well I have been firing for the last six hours, and I am lame and sick and I can't fight any more," we then let him pass on. If the eleventh army corps had stood their ground, we would have had the secesh in a tight place. It was on the third of May that the hardest fighting took place. Our Brigade was under a crossfire of three different batteries, the shells came from the front, rear, and left; our brigade was the last to leave the field; we held our position full one hour and a half too long, as the General could not get one orderly to where we was. He sent three, or started them, but they never reached us.

We lost out of our company five killed and eight wounded, the regiment lost about a hundred men. We fell back across the Rappahannock the day before yesterday.

I remain truly,
William Seufert [13]

[The *Official Roster of Ohio Soldiers* spells the name as Senfert. Pvt. William Senfert was 19 years old when he mustered into the 7th Ohio on October 11, 1861 for three years. The only notation for Senfert is that he "Transferred to [a] detachment of recruits – No further record found."]

In its casualty report, titled "The Old Seventh," the Warren *Western Reserve Chronicle* reported 1 dead, 15 wounded, and 5 missing for Company H. One of the wounded was Samuel H. Barnum who was severely wounded in the bowels. Barnum's struggle to live came to an end on May 22nd.

Samuel H. Barnum; 7th Regiment

Samuel H. Barnum, son of Hiram Barnum, Esq., of Braceville, died in Hospital, at Washington, D.C., on the 22 inst, aged 25 years.

Mr. Barnum first enlisted in Capt. Barrett's company, 19th Regiment O.V., in the three months' service, and fought gallantly in the battle of Rich Mountain, and all others in which his regiment was engaged. When the new regiments were being raised last summer, he received a recruiting commission as Lieutenant, conditioned upon his raising twenty-five men within ten days. He enlisted sixteen for the 7th Regiment, eight for the 19th, and two for the 24th – twenty-six in all, but because he had not enlisted them all for one regiment, he failed to receive his commission, although he had the highest recommendations, and at once enlisted with his sixteen men, at their request, in the 7th. In the arduous campaign of the past winter in which the 7th Regiment bore so conspicuous a part, he won the respect and esteem of his fellow soldiers by his kindness of heart, manliness, and unflinching bravery.

At the battle of Chancellorsville, on the 2d inst., the 7th Regiment was lying to the front, near to, and behind a ridge of land, and from that position, Capt. McClelland,) who had command of the Regiment) was unable to see where to direct his fire, and here they were lying for some time. At length, Capt. McClelland called for three men out of Co. H to volunteer to ascertain where the enemy were. Samuel H. Barnum, William Hunter, and David Wintersteen sprang forward and advanced about two rods, when Hunter was shot through the wrist, and Barnum through the side, as he was retreating to his company – Wintersteen only remaining unhurt. The Regiment had 420 men on the march, most of them being in the fight, a few being on picket duty, and a few detailed for train guard; out of this number eighty-seven were killed, wounded and missing.

The remains of Mr. B. were brought home by his father, and the funeral took place at his residence in Braceville, on Sunday last, attended by a large concourse of people, who were addressed briefly, and to the purpose, by Col. J. F. Asper, and Mrs. Mercia Boynton Lane. He was buried with military honors, the Warren Firemen (of whom he was formerly a member) tendering their services on the occasion.

He leaves a widow – a daughter of Robert M. Miller, Esq., of this place – and an infant daughter. [14]

After the Battle of Chancellorsville, the 7th Ohio remained in camp at Aquia Creek for 36 days. Correspondence from the regiment to the newspapers ceased or else it was by-passed for reports of more urgent events. Aside from meeting their physical comforts and needs, it was certainly a time for the 7th Ohio to reflect on many matters.

Being from Ohio, the men were quite concerned about the furor that arose over the Clement Vallandigham case. The vociferous Peace Democrat and ex-congressman was an idol of the Copperheads and other such groups who opposed the war and the Lincoln administration.

The other part of the situation was the bumbling Gen. Ambrose Burnside who had been shuttled to the Department of the Ohio when Hooker became commander of the Army of the Potomac. Burnside considered the anti-war sentiment as being treasonous. He issued his General Order Number 38, which threatened arrest for treasonous behavior, including anti-war speeches.

Vallandigham took Number 38 as a direct challenge, and he responded to it in an anti-war speech at Mount Vernon, Ohio on May 1, 1863, the same day that Union men were falling in battle at Chancellorsville. Consequently, Vallandigham was arrested at his home in Dayton. The military trial lasted from May 6-16, and Vallandigham was found guilty of treason. On May 19, the War Department ordered Vallandigham to be sent outside of the Union's military boundaries, and on the 25th he was turned over to the Confederates in Tennessee.

It was a sensational case, and the verdict was amazingly swift. For those who were for prosecuting the war, Clement Vallandigham was a detestable and evil figure; but for the Peace Democrats in Ohio and elsewhere, he had become a hero and martyr. On June 11, 1863, Vallandigham, while in absentia, was overwhelmingly voted the gubernatorial nomination of the Peace Democrats in a convention at Columbus. [15] The festering civil discontent would eventually erupt into violence which would directly involve the Seventh Ohio.

On the 27th of May, the 7th Ohio received some newsprint, but it was due to a 5th Ohio correspondent.

General Tyler and Colonel Creighton.

A Fifth Ohio correspondent writes from near Acquia Creek to the Cincinnati Times as follows:

"We were glad to see our old and tried commander, General Tyler, who was on his way home, his brigade's time being up. He always was the favorite of our brigade, and we hope his future command may have as high an estimation of him as that which he led at Port Republic. [Gen. Tyler's military service continued. He served under Gen. Lew Wallace on July 9, 1864 in the Union's delaying action against Jubal Early's Confederates at the Monacacy River near Frederick, Maryland.] Our brigade is now commanded by Colonel Creighton, of the 7th Ohio. He is the right man in the right place, and he never shirks his duty. We could see him everywhere encouraging his men in the engagement of Chancellorsville. He is the style the Fifth like to be under," [16]

As time passed at Aquia Creek, the men of the 7th Ohio had to be wondering which army would make the next move first. Surely, there would be at least one more gigantic battle; it was just a matter of when and where. For those of the 7th Ohio, who had been under fire at Antietam and Chancellorsville, they knew that the next battle would be a horrendous and dreadful ordeal. Hopefully, it would be the last battle of the war. For the maimed and the dead, it was.

On June 3rd, Longstreet's Corps of the Army of Virginia stepped out for the Blue Ridge Mountains, and the invasion of the North was begun. The main task for the Army of the Potomac was to interpose itself between the invading Confederates and Washington, D.C.

Ten days after the initial rebel movement – June 13th – the 12th Corps was ordered to move from Aquia Creek to Dumfries. The 7th Ohio left at 8:00 P.M. and marched ten miles through the darkness. They arrived early in the morning on the 14th and rested.

On June 15th the corps moved to Fairfax Court House on an exhausting 20 mile march. It was hot and humid; a cloud of dust hung over the column of shuffling men, plodding horses and mules, and trundling wagons. With a 14 pound musket, a canteen of water, 40 rounds of ammunition in the cartridge box, a haversack filled with rations, a knapsack filled with personal items, each man in his itchy wool uniform was carrying about 48 pounds on his person. [17] Straps cut into their shoulders, and the sweat ran profusely off their bodies. Fifteen men in Geary's division died of sunstroke this day.

The 16th was a day for resting and rounding up the stragglers from the previous day's march.

They were back to marching on the 17th – a ten mile hike to

Dranesville. The next day their bodies underwent a twelve mile march.

In the previous month, when President Lincoln was reponding to the opposition to Vallandigham's arrest, he answered with the question, "Must I shoot a simple-minded soldier who deserts and not touch a hair of the wily agitator who induces him to desert?" June 19th was a day for shooting those deserters, whether they were influenced by Vallandigham or not. The 12th Corps witnessed the execution of three deserters, and the 7th Ohio was among those who filed past the lifeless bodies. It was a loathsome object lesson.

The fox and hound chase continued on the 26th when the Twelfth Corps crossed the Potomac River at Edward's Ferry, marched through Poolesville, and moved to Monacacy – a march of 9 ½ miles.

The immediate concern for the 7th Ohio on June 27th was the 7-mile trek through Point of Rocks, Maryland and onto Petersville. Meanwhile, Gen. Hooker asked to be relieved of his command. The main issue was the 10,000 man garrison at Harpers Ferry. Hooker wanted the men for the impending battle. The President and his advisor, Gen. Halleck, refused the request. Lincoln wasted no time in accepting Hooker's resignation. [19]

On Sunday, June 28th, while the 7th Ohio was on a 12 mile march to Frederick, Gen. George Gordon Meade assumed command of the Army of the Potomac. From Frederick City to Taneytown is about 22 miles, and on the 29th the Seventh Ohio covered most of the distance. Eighteen miles beyond Taneytown lay Gettysburg, which served as the hub for many spoke-like roads.

On June 30th, the grueling march resumed. Taneytown was passed, and the regiment arrived at Littlestown in the afternoon. It was probably at this time that the 7th Ohio was read Gen. Meade's circular to the army. The General's personality was such that he had earned the sobriquet of the "Ol' Snapping Turtle." If the General's message was meant to inspire as well as to show the gravity of the situation, it appeared to be more gravity than inspiration, especially when it came to the part where "the Corps and other commanders are authorized to order the instant death of any soldier who fails in his duty at this hour." [20]

On July 1st the regiment moved from Littlestown to Two Taverns. The thunder of cannon could be heard in the distance. The ball had begun. Shortly after 1:00 P.M. the 7th Ohio was ordered for-

The 7th Ohio and the Union troops attacked Lookout Mt. in a spiral fashion, coming out of the valley to the right, passing under the sheer palisades, and ascending the mountain to the left of the photo. This is an Eastern National postcard of Lookout Mt., published by Coastal Exposures Inc., Maine.

ward. By five o'clock they occupied a position to the right of and near Little Round Top. During the day the Confederates had driven the Union troops off Seminary Ridge, through Gettysburg, and back to the heights on which the Union Army now perched.

In the early morning hours of July 2nd, Geary's Division was shifted to the extreme right of the line at Culp's Hill. During the day the Seventh constructed substantial breastworks. Tremendous firing erupted on the left of the Union line where the Seventh had been in the early morning hours. Someone else had to face Longstreet's Corps, which had swarmed over the Peach Orchard and Devil's Den and threatened Little Round Top. It was a desperate fight which would determine if the Union line broke or if it remained to fight another day. Geary's Division was ordered to the left to help repulse Longstreet's attack, but the division lost its way in all of the confusion and battle smoke. Fortunately, the Union line held. Geary's Division was ordered back to its original position only to find that the enemy now occupied the breastworks that the Union boys had built.

The fighting around Culp's Hill began in earnest at dawn of July 3rd. It lasted until 11:00 A.M. When the worst cannonading and clash of infantry occurred in the afternoon, it was essentially at the backs of Geary's Division due to its position on the end of the fishhook-shaped Union line. [21]

Letter from One of the 7th.

The following letter was written by a young man who has been in the gallant 7th Ohio Regiment from its first organization. He has been in nearly, if not all, the hard fought battles in which that regiment has participated, and has been so very fortunate as to have thus far escaped uninjured, while so many of his comrades have fallen. The writer of the subjoined letter was employed in this office [*Morning Leader*] as a printer for several years previous to the war, and we are glad to know he has got along so fortunately, and although quite young, has proven himself a brave and faithful soldier. The letter was not written for publication, having been sent to J. M. Stull, Esq., to whom we are indebted for its use.

On the Field of Battle, Gettysburg,
July 4th, 1863.

Dear Uncle: -- I have much that I would like to write at this moment, but there is so much going on that I do not know what to say. This, of course, convinces you that I am safe. In fact we lost but few men. The enemy advanced upon our position; we being on the right flank of the army, and our corps held them in check some- thing like one day. When night came on, the firing ceased, and this morning they have given up the ground, which is found to be covered with dead and wounded, the former by the thousand. We have picked up in our front some 4,000 small arms that the enemy left on the field.

The force which we engaged was Gen. Jackson's old corps, now under command of Gen. Ewell. Jackson's old division were nearly all killed, and the rest taken prisoners, by our division. It was under the command of Gen. Ed. Johnston.

This battle has been the greatest of the war, and the rebs never received such terrible blows before as those which have been given during the last two days, and I think it will result in their almost annihilation or capture before they reach Virginia again. On our left flank, the main part of their army was whipped and thousands upon thousands killed. Yesterday afternoon we took over ten thousand prisoners in one haul. They were badly wounded and cut up before they could come to tea. General Longstreet, the idol of the South, was taken by them, badly wounded in the leg, and died before night. [This bit of misinformation was strictly rumor, or else another Confederate officer was thought to be Longstreet by the hopeful Union soldiers.] It would be hard to tell the amount of prisoners we have taken, they are so numerous, while we have lost but few men. [The correspondent must not have viewed or heard of the carnage that the Confederates wreaked upon the Union Army on the first and second days of the battle. This was only the first day after the major fighting stopped at Gettysburg; and it is most likely that the correspondent had not gone sight-seeing yet.] The rebel is said to be awfully discouraged and will not be able to stand another battle. Our cavalry have done much damage to their wagon train, and is at work on their flanks to-day. This, is to us, [sic] is really a merry Fourth of July. I cannot tell you what we are about to do. This is such a big machine to run that it is hard to tell what is going on. So I hope you will excuse this hasty scratch. I shot about one hundred rounds yesterday.

J. H. MERRILL [22]

J. H. Merrill was correct in his assessment of the relatively light damage to the 7th Ohio. Except for the fight at Culp's Hill on the third day of the battle, they had been fortunate to be ordered out of harm's way. The 7th Ohio arrived at Gettysburg with 265 men and left with 247. One man was killed and 17 were wounded.[23]

Merrill's use of the phrase, "merry Fourth of July," was undoubted used in the context of being relieved that the battle was over and that the Union Army had prevailed. July 4, 1863 was anything but merry. In three days the Union suffered 3,072 killed, 14,497 wounded, and 5,434 missing. The Confederate Army lost 2,592 killed, 12,709 wounded, and more than 5,000 missing or captured. The carnage of wrecked equipment, dismembered horses and mules, and mangled human bodies were strewn all over the landscape. A drizzling rain began at noon and turned into a torrential downpour. It was as if Heaven was profusely weeping over the ghastly folly of mankind. [24]

[The *Official Roster of Ohio Soldiers* listed Private James H. Merrell (sic) as being 18 years old when he mustered into the 7th Ohio on June 20, 1861. Pvt. Merrill only had four and a half months to live. His luck ran out at Ringgold, Georgia on November 11, 1863.]

Ten days after the Battle of Gettysburg, the *Cleveland Morning Leader* reported on the fighting quality of the Ohio troops who had fought at Gettysburg. As the Cleveland newspaper was interested in Ohio soldiers, so the Philadelphia newspaper followed the men from its home state. Gens. Meade and Geary were both Pennsylvanians. Prior to the Civil War, Geary had been an attorney, civil engineer, a Colonel in the War with Mexico, Mayor of San Francisco, and Governor of the Kansas Territory. Geary's impressive background was enhanced by his imposing stature at six feet five and a half inches tall.

General Geary's Brigade of Ohio Troops.

The Ohio troops in the Army of the Potomac, including the 7th, 29th, and 66th regiments, are in a brigade of Geary's division. A correspondent of the Philadelphia Press, writing of the battle, says that the general's 1st brigade, composed of four regiments of Ohio troops, and two of Pennsylvania, commanded by the brave Colonel Candy, of the 66th Ohio, was conspicuous for its steadiness and unflinching front. The correspondent further says:

"During the temporary withdrawal of the 1st division of the 12th corps from the entrenchments they had occupied the night previous, the wily foe had taken advantage of their absence and thrown a whole division, numbering seven thousand men, into the gap. They had taken possession of our breastwork and thrown the greater portion of their force around the right flank and to the rear of General Geary's division. This was affected under cover of darkness. It became at once absolutely necessary to dislodge them. The accomplishment of this object was confided to general Geary. Quietly and with great celerity, he posted his artillery in a position to enfilade them. Troops were massed on both sides of them, and lying down upon their arms were ordered to keep perfectly still until daylight approached.

Before the morning had fully dawned, the struggle commenced. Our boys fought like madmen. General Geary himself superintended the direction of the artillery fire, in order that his own men, who were secreted in the woods, should not suffer by it. [Perhaps, Geary wanted to avoid the "friendly fire" which hit his troops at Chancellorsville.]

From four o'clock until 10 A.M., the contest was waged with unparalleled fury, and then the enemy fled precipitately, falling back beyond the line of fire, and leaving us masters of the position. General Geary was promptly reinforced during the action by General Meade, who sent a brigade of tried men from the 6th corps, under command of General Shaler, for that purpose. They fully maintained their enviable reputation as fighting men. General Meade complimented General Geary and the 12th Corps for the success of this undertaking. [25]

As Gen. Lee's battered army retreated toward the Potomac River, the Union cavalry harassed the wagon trains and sparred with the Confederate rear guard. The recent rains had swollen the Potomac so that Lee was trapped. However, Gen. Meade cautiously herded his infantry and artillery toward the rebel army. By the time the Union Army was in position to do further damage to, if not completely bag, the Army of Northern Virginia, the river subsided; and during the night of July 13th, the rebels completed their withdrawal across the river. Instead of ending the war, it was the beginning of nearly 22 more months of suffering and bloodshed.

To Gen. Meade, a native Pennsylvanian, the Union Army under his command had driven "the invaders from our soil." To President Abraham Lincoln's way of thinking, everything from the Great Lakes to the Gulf of Mexico was *our* soil. [26]

One would expect a large volume of soldier-to-newspaper correspondence following Gettysburg, such as that which followed Antietam; but this was not the case in northern Ohio. One reason may have been that such a notion was "played out" with the fighting men who were exhausted and more hardened after this colossal bloodletting.

From the standpoint of the newspapers, there was a plethora of important news to report. Not only was the Battle of Gettysburg important news, but the tidings of Grant's victory at Vicksburg and Pemberton's surrender on July 4th began to cross the telegraph wires. Events peculiar to Ohio also vied with the aforementioned battles. On July 8th, Gen. John Morgan's Confederate Cavalry crossed the Ohio River into Indiana. The raiders headed east.

From the Union point of view there was little glamour and chivalry in Morgan's Raid. Killing citizens and ruthlessly destroying non-military property was the kind of behavior for which the Union cavalry would be condemned, not glorified.

Aside from the fighting that resulted in the chase of Morgan's Raiders, some odd depredations were conducted by the rebels. One William Parker (the great-great grandfather of the author's wife, Lora) eventually filed a claim with the State of Ohio for property taken, destroyed, or injured by the raiders. Parker lost 30 dozen sheaves of wheat at $15, 1 pitcher for 75 cents, and fourteen pounds of cheese at 10 cents a pound for $1.40, for a total of $17.15. William's brother Daniel, who also lived near Rutland, Ohio, was ehit harder by Morgan's men. He reported the loss of a horse worth $125, damage to trees and crops valued at $25, corn and wheat at $10, one drum at $4, and a linen coat at $2, which totaled $166. William Parker was eventually awarded $13 on his claim; and Daniel Parker was allotted $135.[27]

Until Morgan's capture with a remnant of his troops on July 26th at New Lisbon, Ohio, the state's newspapers printed reams of fact, fiction, and rumors regarding Morgan's raiders.

In Ohio the continuing saga of Clement Vallandigham also furnished an abundance of newsprint; only this time the resistance to the impending draft was intertwined with that story. On March 3, 1863, Congress passed the Enrollment Act, which called for federally controlled conscription. Of the 22 loyal states, Ohio's quota ranked third in "The Draft." New York was first with an apportionment of 71,010; Pennsylvania followed with 58,280 and Ohio with 42,180.[28]

In Ohio and elsewhere there had always been pockets where the local majority of the people adhered to a political philosophy contrary to that of the Lincoln administration. Holmes County, Ohio was one such place where the Democratic Party prevailed from a traditional standpoint as well as a heartfelt belief that the war was precipitated by the abolitionist agitation and prolonged by a tyrannical government. To oppose the federally mandated draft was a natural development.

Holmes County also harbored many members of the Knights of the Golden Circle, a secret society of the Copperhead variety. These anti-war Democrats were further irritated when Vallandigham was arrested, tried, and convicted for treason. The editor of the *Holmes County Farmer* had even endorsed Vallandigham for the presidency.[29]

The situation in Holmes County began to seethe when a draft officer began searching the steep hills of the area. He was chased off with a flurry of rocks and threatened with death if he ever returned. The officer reported the incident to the provost marshal who later arrested four of the ringleaders. However, these Peace Democrats were not of the passive stripe. On June 5th, while the ringleaders were being marched off to captivity, a group of 60-70 armed resisters menacingly confronted the provost marshal and compelled him to release the prisoners.

A report of the civil disobedience was sent to Columbus. In short order, Gov. Tod sent Col. William Wallace and 420 men to Holmes County to subdue the uprising. On June 17th, the soldiers deployed and moved on the rebels' stronghold. Bushwhackers opened fire, and the soldiers retaliated. Two bushwhackers were killed, 3 wounded, and several captured. Later in the day, a citizens committee approached Col. Wallace to see what could be done to prevent further bloodshed. The citizens were given an ultimatum to hand over the four ringleaders in 24 hours, which was done on the night of June 18th. "So ended the 'Holmes County Rebellion' or as it has been dubbed by many, the "Battle of Fort Fizzle." [30]

In all fairness, it is obligatory to note that many Holmes County Democrats fought in the Union Army. Some of them gave their lives for the Union cause, and their names would be forever memorialized on an impressive monument next to the courthouse in Millersburg.

Although the 7th Ohio had their minds on the impending battle in mid-June, these festering draft problems would have a direct bearing on the Seventh's near future.

The "Holmes County Rebellion" was minuscule compared to the draft riot that erupted in New York City on July 13, 1863. At the heart of the problem was the agitation over the $300 clause of the Enrollment Act, which allowed a man to purchase a substitute. Vallandigham, New York politicians, and dissenters interpreted this clause as an unfair discrimination against the poor. [31] Thus, the Civil War, as well as some future wars, was characterized as being a rich man's war and a poor man's fight.

The trouble in New York City had been fomenting since the Enrollment Act was passed in early March, but when the draft wheel was set in motion on the morning of July 13th, the volatile situation began to escalate into a full-scale riot.

... From the Evening Post of Monday we quote the following particulars of the riot:
PARTICULARS OF THE RIOT – THE DRAFT RE-

COMMENCED.

The drawing by Provost Marshal Jenkins did not commence punctually at 9 o'clock this morning, as we intended. The Provost Marshal had received intimations that riotous demonstrations were probable, and he accordingly sent to Acting Assistant Provost-Marshal General Nugent and the police for a force which would be sufficient to suppress any disorder.

At 10 o'clock, however, although orders had been given to the military and to the police of the different wards, no assistance had arrived except ten or twelve policemen. The Provost Marshal at that hour decided to commence the drawing. The great wheel was placed upon the table, the blindfolded man took his position beside it; the man at the wheel was ready to perform his duty, and the Provost Marshal announced that the draft in the Twenty-second ward, which was begun on Saturday, would then be concluded. The wheel began to revolve amid the somewhat demonstrations of the crowd of spectators (numbering from one to two hundred persons); and the draft proceeded for about twenty minutes, when the more formidable riot took place. [32]

The angry crowd quickly escalated to a wild mob of over 50,000, most of them Irish workmen and the poor of their neighborhoods. The ensuing reign of anarchy and terror lasted for four days.[33] Traffic was stopped and the horses were released from their vehicles. Fights broke out with the undermanned policemen, some of whom were brutally beaten to death. Offices of the provost marshals were put to the torch, and the firemen were driven off. Pistol shots whizzed through the air. Negroes were attacked, some were hanged along the streets, and a "Colored Orphan Asylum" was burnt to the ground. Looting was widespread. [34]

On July 15th, the *Cleveland Morning Leader* expressed its views of the ongoing riot in New York City.

... The telegraph brings additional reports from the

fearful draft riot in New York. The scenes of carnage, outrage, arson and bloodshed of Monday were continued yesterday. The merchants, brokers, &c., were organizing for the defense. Numerous houses were fired. The rioters were in several instances fired upon by troops. Governor Seymour made a speech to the crowd, saying that he had sent to Washington to endeavor to have the draft *stopped*. We hope he will not succeed, because it would be giving a lawless mob prestige of victory which would not fail to strengthen and encourage similar manifestations there and elsewhere...
MEASURES FOR SUPPRESSING THE RIOT.
General Wool and the authorities at the Brooklyn Navy Yard have been notified of the disturbances, and a large force of United States Marines, besides a considerable number of soldiers of the regular army, have been ordered into instant service.
The Responsibility for the Riot.
A fearful riot has been running wild in New York. Property has been destroyed, laws outraged, public safety imperiled, and many lives lost; all sacrifices to a brutal, beastly, irresponsible *mob*. Where is the responsibility? The question is easily answered. The authors of the riot are not the authorities who ordered the draft in pursuance of the requirements of the National Legislature; but Copperhead speakers and writers who have incited the unreasoning, passionate masses, to these deeds of violence. This assertion needs no argument. It is plain as noonday, and if the men of this day or they of any future generation seek proof of this charge they will find it in the speeches that were made in New York City on Thursday last, and in the files of the Democratic papers before and since that day ... [35]

Eventually, troops from Gettysburg were called in to keep a lid on the rioting mob. In the aftermath of the New York draft riot, there were over 1,000 dead and wounded. [36]

The 7th Ohio began the long trek back to Virginia, marching from 8 to 21 miles per day, except for an occasional day of rest. As the footsore soldiers marched along the Potomac River, dead Confederates could be seen floating down the river. On the positive side in an infantryman's life, the weather in the last half of July was quite pleasant; and since it was blackberry picking time, many regiments received an added treat when they stopped to rest or camp at night.[37]

By August 1st, the Seventh was back across the Rappahannock River. For the next two weeks, the regiment endured the dog days of summer. It was intensely hot during the day.

The New York draft was rescheduled for August 31 and September 7. To the detriment of the Union's offensive plans, many regiments were sent to New York to head off any potential trouble. One of the lucky regiments was the 7th Ohio. On August 16th, the men marched to Rappahannock Station where they boarded the train for Alexandria.[38]

The men of the 4th Ohio were headed for the same destination as the Seventh. While in Alexandria, the men of the Fourth were flush with a recent pay, so they boarded at hotels and restaurants. For a quarter they could dine on thick slabs of ham and eat all of the eggs that their stomachs could hold. Their ravenous appetites put a dent in the supplies of the local pig sties and chicken coops.[39]

On August 27th, the Seventh boarded the ocean steamer, Baltic, "which was novel and interesting to the great mass of the soldiers, who had never before seen a boat of such huge dimensions." The regiment sailed down the Potomac and thence to New York where they spent a pleasant week on Governor's Island. Since the draft took place peacefully, it was like a vacation for the 7th Ohio. They re-embarked on the Baltic and sailed back to Alexandria. By September 17th, the regiment was back with Geary's Division near Raccoon Ford on the Rapidan River.[40]

Chapter Six

"Let us have the 7th back"

In early September of 1863, Gen. R. E. Lee and the Confederate Government again initiated a move, which would spark another chain of events. On September 9-10, Gen. James Longstreet and his veteran corps of about 11,000 troops boarded the trains and headed west to join Gen. Braxton Bragg's army in Tennessee. By the time Longstreet's corps arrived, the Union's Gen. William Rosecrans had maneuvered Bragg to the south of Chattanooga and across the Georgia line near a stream called Chickamauga Creek.

When the intelligence of Longstreet's departure was received and verified some days later, the Federals responded by sending 16,300 soldiers from the Army of the Potomac to join Rosecran's army in the west. Much of the 11th Corps under Gen. O. O. Howard and all of the 12th Corps under Gen. Henry W. Slocum made up this force. Gen. Joseph Hooker headed the entire command. Within this array of troops was the 7th Ohio in Gen. John Geary's division.

Before the Union reinforcements under Hooker could get under away, Longstreet had already linked up with Bragg; and the Confederates turned on Rosecran's pursuing Union Army. The bloody Battle of Chickamauga was fought on September 19-20. Confederate casualties numbered 18,454 with 2,300 of that total killed. The Federals suffered 16,170 casualties with 1,600 of them killws. Except for Gen. George Thomas' determined resistance, Rosecran's army broke and made a disorderly retreat to Chattanooga. The Confederates cautiously pursued and put Chattanooga under siege. Now the objective for Hooker's force was to help save Rosecran's army from starvation.

The time delay in ascertaining Longstreet's departure from the Army of Northern Virginia accounted for much of the Union tardiness in reaching Rosecrans. Clearing the usual governmental red tape, organizing the troops to be sent west, and arranging for transportation and commissary needs added further delays. It wasn't until September 26th that the 7th Ohio marched to Bealton, Virginia. On the following day, the regiment boarded the cars for the move west. It would take 34 days to transport the 7th Ohio and the Union forces under Hooker to the vicinity of Chattanooga. [1]

The first stop for the 7th Ohio was at Washington, D.C. where the regiment left the cars for an hour to shop for "wet and dry goods." On September 30th, the Seventh arrived at Benwood, Virginia on the Ohio River. They crossed over to Bellaire, Ohio and arrived at Columbus on the evening of October 1st. Indianapolis was reached on the 2nd and Louisville on the 3rd. The regiment arrived in Nashville, Tennessee on October 5th.

One reason for the slow passage of Hooker's force south of the Ohio River was the constant harassment of the Confederate cavalry and the guerrillas who destroyed the railroad tracks and burned the bridges. One such incident occurred at Duck River Bridge on the way to Wartrace. The train carrying the 7th and 66th Ohio regiments was halted by a band of rebel bridge burners. The two regiments were ordered to leave the cars and to disperse the enemy. Col. John Colburn, 33rd Indiana and commanding the 3rd Brigade, reported: "Of the conduct of the officers and men of the Seventh and Sixty-sixth Ohio Regiments I can speak in the highest commendation. They obeyed all commands to form and advance upon the enemy with promptness, activity, and order." Nevertheless, it took six hours to rebuild the bridge. [2]

By October 13th, the 7th Ohio was in Wartrace where they voted unanimously in favor of Republican John Brough for Governor of Ohio. There were many Democrats in the regiment, but the thought of voting for a Copperhead was abhorrent.

At this time, Lt. Col. Crane of the Seventh was at his home in Cleveland where he also voted. The *Morning Leader* carried the following patriotic and somewhat humorous item on its front page for October 15th.

A PATRIOTIC GIRL. – Lieutenant-Colonel Crane, of the noble Seventh, who has been home for a day or two, left last night, after casting a vote for the Union, to rejoin his regiment. With him went his wife and her sister, Miss Hutton. It appeared that the carriage which called for them had been used by the Copperheads for electioneering purposes, and still bore the label, – now played out forever – "Vallandigham and Pugh." On reading this, Miss Hutton stepped up to the carriage at once, and tore away the placard, exclaiming, "I can never go a step under that motto, – *never.*"

Let us remember, in our joy, the loyal *women* of Ohio. To their influence we owe many a vote which has been thrown to swell the majority for our gallant leader. [3]

While the Seventh continued its slow train ride to Bridgeport, Alabama, dramatic changes occurred in the command structure of the Union's western army. Gen. Ulysses Grant replaced Gen. Rosecrans on October 16th. Grant had a reputation of always vigorously coming to grips with the enemy. He arrived in Chattanooga on the 24th.

The first task for Grant was to open the "cracker line." Although the men were on short rations, no deaths due to starvation were reported. As for the horses and mules, it was a different story; their emaciated carcasses were strewn all over the Chattanooga area. The main problem was that the Confederates on the heights controlled the easiest access route to the town.

On October 26th, Hookers' troops crossed the Tennessee River at Bridgeport and headed east toward Wauhatchie and Brown's Ferry. The next phase of the operation began at three o'clock in the morning on the 27th. Gen. William B. Hazen, a Portage County man, and 1,800 men silently moved into the river with 60 pontoons and floated downstream undetected by the enemy's pickets. At 5:00 A.M., Hazen's men landed at Brown's Ferry on the other side of the river and captured most of the rebel pickets. Gen. William F. Smith, who headed the amphibious operation, had taken the remaining 2,200 men on a circular route behind the hills to the point across from Brown's Ferry. By 7:00 A.M. Smith's force was ferried across the river; and by 10:00 A.M. the pontoon bridge was laid. On the afternoon of October 28th, Gen. Howard's 11th Corps marched to Brown's Ferry and linked up with the Union forces there. Now, rather than supplying the Union Army by the backbreaking and inefficient route over the mountains, all of the much-needed supplies could be easily brought to this point on the river and thence to Chattanooga. The "cracker line" was now open. The next step for Grant was to lift the siege and to get at Bragg's army.

The Confederates tried to break the Union line near Brown's Ferry on the night of October 28th and into the early morning hours. In this rare night attack, Longstreet's Corps attacked Geary's Division, which was located three miles from Brown's Ferry. At Wauhatchie,

"Geary had been engaged for about three hours against a vastly superior force. The night was so dark that the men could not distinguish one from another except by the light of the flashes of their muskets ... By four o'clock in the morning the battle had entirely ceased, and our "cracker line" was never afterward disturbed." – U. S. Grant. [5]

The second task for Grant was to build up his hungry army; and supplies poured into Chattanooga. Additional Union troops continued to flow into the area; Gen. William Sherman's 17,000 men were at Bridgeport after making the long trek from Memphis.

The original Union battle plan was to have Sherman's men make the main thrust from the Union left. In the early morning hours of November 24th, the Union forces skillfully and stealthily crossed the Tennessee River. After initial success, the attack stalled due to the rugged terrain and the gutsy, stubborn resistance of the rebels.

At the center of the line was Gen. George Thomas' Army of the Cumberland, which was itching to avenge their defeat near the banks of Chickamauga Creek. Thomas' men were to pressure Bragg's center so he could not reinforce the rebel flanks. No one ever dreamed that Thomas' men could take the steep mountainside of Missionary Ridge by frontal assault; nevertheless, the common soldiers on their own volition stormed the heights and broke the center of Bragg's line. On the Union right, Hooker was to take Lookout Mountain and to secure the valley between the heights. The latter operation involved Geary's Division and the 7th Ohio.

Early in the morning on November 24th, Hooker sent Geary's Division and a brigade up Lookout Creek to effect a crossing. A bridge near the railroad crossing was seized while Geary's men continued further upstream. A heavy mist at the top of the mountain obscured Geary from the Confederate troops, so they easily crossed the creek and captured forty pickets. Then the assault began on the steep, rugged, heavily timbered, and chasmed mountain. [6] The Union maneuver was similar to a clockwise spiral that kept them under the sheer cliffs and away from the Confederate artillery, which could not be depressed at that angle.

At 1:00 P.M. on the 24th, Geary sent the following message to Gen. Daniel Butterfield, Hooker's Chief of Staff: "General: We are nearly on the crest of the hill. Everything is successful so far. The enemy holds the crest in considerable force against us." Fifteen minutes later, Geary sent another message: "General: We are immed-

The distance from Chattanooga to Allatoona and Pumpkin Vine Creek is 90.5 miles over very rugged terrain.

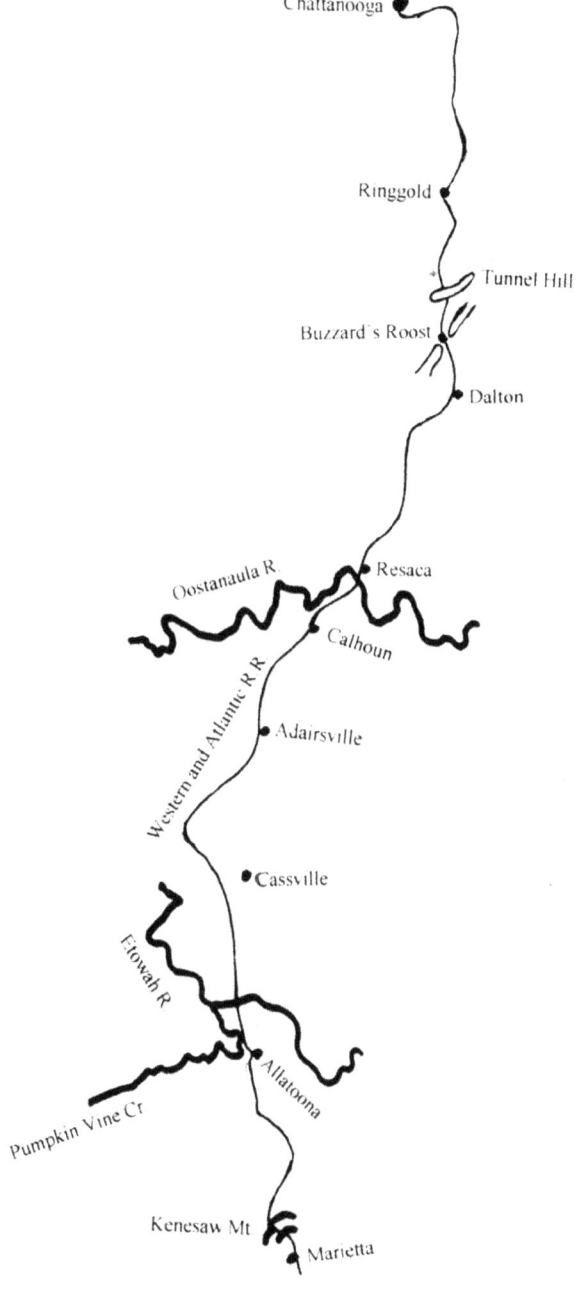

iately under the crest of the hill. We have between 300 and 400 prisoners, and have taken two pieces of artillery. Please send me artillerists to work them." [7]

Hooker's headquarters were in Lookout Valley. At 2:00 P.M. he responded to Geary: "Make yourself strong in the position you occupy tonight. I am on the Chattanooga road, and do not know that I will be able to communicate with you personally to-night. Our men are out removing trees and other obstructions." [8]

By 2:45 P.M. Geary was getting anxious. "General: We are pressed heavily, and need re-enforcements. We must have ammunition; I have sent for some, but it does not come. My rear should be well looked to." To this harried message, a self-assured Hooker responded at 4:00 P.M.: "After the fog lifts I expect to descend into the valley, unless I receive orders to the contrary. The force I have there now should be able to hold it until that time. Our communications on the left with Chattanooga is established. In all probability the enemy will evacuate to-night. His line of retreat is seriously threatened by my troops." At 4:50 P.M., Hooker again communicated with Geary. "I congratulate you and your command on their glorious achievements of to-day. As the upper part of the line is exposed, it has been stiffened with re-enforcements. ..." [9]

At daylight on November 25, 1863, Gen. Geary sent the following message directly to his superior:

> Major-General Hooker:
> I have the honor to inform you that our flag waves over the peak of Lookout Mountain.
> Very respectfully, your obedient servant,
> JNO. W. GEARY,
> Brigadier General, Commanding. [10]

At 10:00 on the same morning, the 7th Ohio descended Lookout Mountain. [11] The regiment marched with Geary's Division through Rossville, and around dusk they were near Graysville. Along the way the pursuing Union troops could see the evidence of a fleeing enemy; smoke from burning wagons and supplies, broken caissons, abandoned ammunition, tents, and camp equipment were strewn along the route. Progress during the day over the rugged terrain was further impeded by the burning bridges that the enemy left behind them.

At daylight on November 27th, Geary's Division marched from their bivouac and headed for Ringgold. At 8:00 A.M. the command marched hurriedly through the town under musketry fire from Taylor Ridge on the other side of town. Here, the rear guard of Bragg's retreating army was under the command of Gen. Patrick Cleburne, a brave and competent Irish fighting man who was intent on punishing the oncoming Yankees, just like he had repelled Sherman in the Battle of Chattanooga. Of vital importance to the retreating Confederates was the narrow gap that ran through Taylor Ridge; so Cleburne had the heights bristling with infantry muskets and the gap defended with masked artillery.

Creighton's brigade, including the 7th Ohio, was sent to the left "to scale the mountain, gain the summit, if possible, attack the enemy in flank, and to charge with vigor along the ridge." It was a tall order to execute. Without artillery support, the impatient Union infantry scurried over the clinging yellow Georgia soil toward the death trap.

Under an accurate and galling fire poured down upon them from the heights 500 feet above with the effect that began to tell upon the ranks, Creighton steadily ascended the steep sides of the hill, resolutely determined to carry it with that sanguineness which prowess had in its many engagements inspired that gallant command ... Volley after volley was poured into the hosts above, and a murderous fire swept back into our own lines ... The Seventh Ohio, on the right of the regiment of the extreme left was compelled to move through a ravine, through which it was rapidly ascending, when a terrific enfilading fire from the enemy quickly massed at that point suddenly rose up, mostly taking effect on this regiment. It received and returned it unflinchingly, and pressed on until some of its skirmishers were near the summit, and the regiment was within less than 25 yards of it. But the enemy, strongly enforced, was overpoweringly superior, with every advantage of position. The skirmishers were repulsed, and the Seventh, having lost its gallant leader, Lieutenant-Colonel Crane, 12 out of 13 of its officers, and nearly one-half its men taken into action being disabled, was retired. It moved back slowly and sullenly, delivering its volleys with coolness, and bringing off as many of its wounded as possible. [12]

As the brigade retired to a sheltered position, Creighton had indeed fell mortally wounded. In his report, Gen. Geary especially commended Creighton, Crane, and their men.

> Col. W. R. Creighton and Lieut. Col. O. J. Crane, of the Seventh Ohio Volunteers, were two as brave men and thorough veterans as ever commanded men in the field. To speak of Creighton and Crane in the command was at once to personify all that was gallant, brave, and daring. Colonel Creighton commanded the First Brigade (to which his regiment was attached) at the time of his death, and Lieutenant-Colonel Crane led the regiment in the assault upon Taylor's Ridge. In this attack the latter was killed in the sight of his regimental commander, whose feelings, at the sudden bereavement, were manifested in one of those sudden ebulitions of the affections that seem out of place on the battlefield, but which reflect the highest credit upon those exhibiting them. Rallying his own regiment, he reformed it in the face of the enemy, and calling upon it to avenge Crane's death and to bring away his body, he [Creighton] led them forward a second time. Shortly afterward he fell, and his last inspiration was characteristic of his brave and noble heart: "Hurrah for the First Brigade! Hurrah for the Union! Tell my wife ---." He was no more. These, and other brave men, are lost to the cause and their country, but as their commander I cannot withhold at this time my own personal tribute to their worth and gallantry. [13]

On September 7th, Monday morning, the *Cleveland Morning Leader* printed a non-commissioned officer's view of the tragedies that he witnessed on Taylor's Ridge near Ringgold, Georgia.

THE BATTLE OF RINGGOLD, GA.
Particulars of the Death of Colonels Creighton and Crane.

The following account of the battle of Ringgold, which closed the four days' fighting that resulted in the complete rout of Bragg's Army, and in the early part of which Colonels Creighton and

Crane fell, will prove interesting to our readers. We are indebted for the facts to Sergeant-Major W. P. Tisdel, who participated throughout, and was near Colonel Creighton when he fell:

About midnight of the 26th of December [November], Geary's Division, having marched during the day from Mission Ridge, where they had been engaged the day before, bivouacked about four miles northwest of Ringgold, in the woods, without tents or blankets, and with a short supply of provisions. Here, the men made the best of their beds upon the cold ground, the arduous march of the day and the fighting they had passed through the two days previous rendering them much fatigued. At five o'clock on the following morning (27th) the order was given to move, and the division took up its line of march toward Ringgold, the route being strewn with the debris of Bragg's Army. – About eight o'clock the division came in sight of Ringgold, but found it could not cross Chickamauga Creek at the point desired, and therefore moved around a bend in the creek to a bridge. This brought them in full sight of the operations at Ringgold, where skirmishers of the opposing forces were engaged. Crossing the bridge, the division entered the town, the 7th in advance, and was halted. During this time the fighting had commenced sharply at Pigeon Gap, where the right of the Federal line rested. About nine o'clock an order came for the 1st Brigade of Geary's Division, Colonel Creighton commanding, to move to the left and assault Pigeon Mountain, the design being to flank the enemy. The brigade was immediately set in motion, and proceeded to the foot of the mountain, where it was formed in line of battle, the 7th on the right. Colonel Creighton then spoke to his command in these words: "Boys, we are ordered to take that hill; I want to see you walk right up it." He thereupon gave the order to forward, and the brigade commenced its march up the hill, when a severe fire was opened upon it from the crest. The brigade, however, pushed on, but had not gone more than a third of the distance until it was found impracticable to proceed further in that direction, whereupon Colonel Creighton obliqued his command to the left to get the benefit of a ravine. Reaching the ravine the brigade again moved towards the top of the hill, and when about two-thirds up were opened upon by a terrific enfilading fire, killing and wounding many. It was at this point that Colonels Creighton and Crane received their death wounds, the ball which killed Colonel Creighton entering the left arm just above the elbow (in the same spot, strange to say, where it did at the time he was wounded at Cedar Mountain,) breaking the arm and entering the side and passing through the body to just beneath the skin on the right side, whence it was extracted. Colonel Crane was shot in the head, the ball entering about two inches above the right ear.

He died instantly, and his body was left on the field until the artillery came up, when the enemy were obliged to give up their position, it was brought off. Colonel Creighton lived some few minutes after receiving his wound, most of the time unconscious. The only words he was heard to utter were, "Oh, my dear wife." His body was promptly taken from the field by members of the Seventh regiment.

About this time the brigade had received orders to fall back, which it did in as good shape as was possible, and was again reformed in the rear of the forces that had occupied the railroad cut at the foot of the mountain. The infantry fire still continued heavy on the right, the fight going on some two hours longer, when the arrival of artillery forced the enemy to retire, and the conflict ceased about four o'clock in the afternoon. Subsequently the brigade was ordered to the position it occupied before the fight, and is now probably at Chickamauga, General Hooker having fallen back to that position.

The loss of the brigade in this most sanguinary encounter was very large, the Seventh sustaining the heaviest loss. All of its officers but one (Captain Creiher, of Company K,) went down before the fire of the enemy, either killed or wounded. Adjutant Baxter, while in the advance of the regiment, received five wounds, which have probably, ere this, proved fatal. When the brigade retired, he was left with Lieutenant-Colonel Crane and some other wounded, in the hands of the enemy. They took him, wounded as he was, over the ridge, stripped him of his clothing, and carried them and whatever else valuable he had about him away with them. It was in this robbed and naked state that Adjutant Baxter was found when our forces had driven the rebels from the ridge, after the final assault. No braver man ever drew his sword in any cause, and his loss to the service cannot but be severely felt ...

[A list of the many killed and wounded of the Seventh was printed. Of the old Franklin Rifles, Company F, "Lieutenant H. A. Spencer, Chardon, wounded in the leg, severe. Sergeant Stratton, John Baptist, William Johnson, (legs) wounded; Oliver Grinnell, killed." Of the old Tyler Guards, Company G, "Captain W. J. Braden, wounded in the leg, severe."] [14]

Col. William Creighton and Lt. Col. Crane were not only brave, heroic Union officers, but they were also Cleveland men; and the citizens were resolved to honor their own. William Creighton had been a printer by trade and a member of the Typographical Union. Orin Crane had been a ship-carpenter. When Fort Sumter was fired on, Creighton raised Company A of the 7th Ohio and became its Captain; Crane was his First Lieutenant. Now their corpses were coming home.

"The remains had been embalmed at Nashville, nearly a week after death, no facilities for such a purpose existing at Chattanooga. The body of Colonel Creighton was not as well as preserved as could be wished, but the remains of Colonel Crane presented a very natural appearance."

When the bodies arrived in Cleveland on Sunday morning, December 6th, a crowd of about 3,000 grieving citizens was at the depot. A military escort accompanied the flag-draped hearse bearing the body of Col. Creighton to his home. All was silent along the route except for the measured tread of the escort, the clip-clop of the horses' hooves, and the slow beat of two muffled drums. The escort returned to the depot to accompany in like manner the body of Lt. Col. Crane to the home of his widow on the west side.

From ten o'clock in the morning to nine o'clock at night on Monday, the bodies lay in state at the Council Hall where the public was admitted to view the dead officers.

On Tuesday, the bodies were escorted from the Council hall to the 1st Presbyterian Church for the funeral ceremony. At 12:30, the funeral procession moved to Erie Street Cemetery while minute guns were fired and the bells in the city tolled. [15]

While the city of Cleveland mourned its dead of Company A, the *Western Reserve Chronicle* was more concerned with its boys who were in Company H.

The 7th Regiment's Wounded.

In the list of wounded of the 7th Regiment at Ringgold, Ga., we observe the name of Jas. H. Merrill of Co. H. [The letter writer after the Battle of Gettysburg] Jimmy had been in nearly every battle in which the 7th had participated, and was one of the very few of that veteran and battle riven regiment that escaped unhurt through its many perils. But his good fortune could not save him amid the tempest of iron hail that cut down Cols. Creighton and Crane, and every commissioned officer but one, in the regiment. – We hope our brave printer soldier will soon be himself again. [It proved to be a vain hope since Jimmy died from his wounds.] ...

Of the 100 men that left Warren in Co. H, at the formation of the Seventh Regiment, but 13 of the original number were left previous to the late battle in Georgia. Of that 13, several are on the list of wounded.

We see there is a proposal made by some of the special friends of the 7th to "bring it home." We doubt whether the few braves that remain of its number would not prefer to serve out the few remaining months of their three years term, but we certainly think their return could not be objected to by any but themselves, and if it is their wish to come home, God speed them. [16]

The sentiment of the *Chronicle* in regard to bringing the 7th Ohio home was expanded upon by the *Cleveland Leader* on the very same day.

Let the Seventh Come Back.

The Herald, in an eloquent and able article, published last evening, proposes that the grand old Seventh, reduced now to a bare hundred men, be, for its good conduct, brought home and mustered out of service.

Of the first part of the proposition we heartily approve. It would be well to have the veterans to come back, and show the colors which they have so honorably upheld on many bloody fields. The spectacle would arouse the military enthusiasm of the [Western] Reserve as Presidential proclamations and speeches from the most eloquent lips would not. About that old flag, rent with the hail of Winchester, Port Republic, Cedar Mountain, Antietam, Chancellorsville, Gettysburg, and Ringgold, the chivalrous youth of the Reserve would rally with the enthusiasm of the early days of the war. It is settled that to be able to say I belonged to the 7th, is, in all time, to be a privilege worth more than all the gold men ever dug. The desire to share with this privilege would con- spire with the ardor which the example of chivalric deeds always excites in bringing recruits to the public cause.

So, then, let us have the 7th back. But let us keep it only, until recruited to the maximum, it shall be able to go back and rehearse in new exploits the valor and enterprise which have made its name immortal. [17]

The official return of casualties for the 7th Ohio in the Chattanooga-Ringgold campaign, November 24-29 inclusive, showed the following:

        Killed – 3 officers, 13 men.
        Wounded – 10 officers, 48 men.
        Aggregate – 74. [18]

Going into the campaign the strength of the regiment was 206 according to Major Wood; therefore the regiment's loss was 36 %. However, taken from the standpoint of leadership, the regiment was severely crippled with the loss of so many officers. This was undoubtedly one of the factors for the depressed mental state of the regiment following Ringgold. Wood, a regimental historian of the Seventh, stated that the regiment's "pride and spirit were broken" after that battle. [19] Lawrence Wilson, another historian of the regiment, recalled that the severe losses at Ringgold for the 7th Ohio caused a great depression in the few officers and men remaining "which never again seemed to be fully obliterated." [20]

In spite of the public clamor, newspaper pleadings, and political pressure from northeast Ohio, the War Department certainly was not inclined to bring any able-bodied soldier home as long as he had any service time remaining. From the Department's view, other regiments in the service of the Union Armies had been as crippled as the 7th Ohio, some even far worse. If the 7th Ohio were allowed to return home, then many other regiments would have to be treated in the same manner. It was a time when the War Department desperately needed men. Volunteering had nearly dried up, and the draft was slow in operation. In short, the Federal Government could ill afford to send anyone home, especially veteran soldiers, not even temporarily.

Chapter Seven

"An outburst of exultation rent the air"

After the bloody repulse on Taylor Ridge, the dispirited and battle-weary 7th Ohio Volunteer Infantry trudged back to the Wauhatchie Valley. Here, they remained in camp until January 4, 1864. On that day the regiment marched to Bridgeport, arriving on the 5th. It was a bleak and dreary season, but Sgt. Lawrence Wilson recalled that "With good quarters, sufficient supplies, and light duty, the stay of the Seventh was altogether pleasant and enjoyable." [1]

Although the physical needs of the Seventh were being satisfied, their collective emotional and mental conditions were in a state of uncertainty. Looking back to the last battle, there was some second-guessing and grousing about how the regiment was handled by the higher brass. It was a time to lament their departed comrades and messmates and to think of the folks at home over Christmas and New Year's Day.

Looking to the future, most of the scuttlebutt around the campfires centered around who would fill the leadership void at all levels, the matter of how much time remained in their term of service, and whether to "veteranize" [reenlist].

The top position in the 7th was filled by an old familiar face, Capt. Frederick A. Seymour of Co. G. Seymour, who had resigned his position on April 23, 1863 on account of disability, was appointed Major on December 1, 1863. Major George Wood thought that Seymour was a brave soldier and a personable man: "Among his fellow soldiers he had many friends, and he will always be remembered as a kind-hearted gentleman." [2]

Sgt. Wilson did not hold Major Seymour in the same light as did Major Wood. Wilson hinted that Seymour was an opportunist who replaced Capt. E. J. Krieger, the only man of that rank in the Seventh to escape harm at Ringgold. According to Wilson, when

Capt. Seymour heard of the death of Col. Creighton and Lt. Col. Crane, he "obtained a commission as major and at once came to the front and assumed command. However, in doing so he became very unpopular with a majority of his officers and men, who made it very unpleasant for him until he resigned" on March 29, 1864. On the other hand, Sgt. Wilson was quite pleased when Capt. Samuel McClellan, "one of the oldest, bravest, and best captains of the regiment, who had been severely wounded in the battle of Ringgold, was commissioned lieutenant-colonel, much to the gratification of his men, and assumed command." [3]

The entire leadership matter was cheerfully summed up in some newspaper correspondence received from Bridgeport on March 30, 1864. The writer's misspelling was apparently over- looked by the editor.

The Seventh Ohio

Have just completed commodious quarters on the site of their former encampment, which indicates that they will be retained here as a portion of the permanent garrison, and I am sure such an order would meet with the approval of all those gallant fellows, now worn down by long and tedious marches. Colonel McClellan has wrought wonderful changes in the general appearance of things since his return, resusitating good feeling and discipline to its former high standard. That gloom which hung pall-like over them during all those dark days of last winter, sorrow has melted away, and its stead a healthy liviness of both body and mind seems to prevale, notwithstanding that they were recently notified that they would be held till June, though their time realy expired [unreadable] of this month, having been mustered in April 25, 1861 and never mustered out since then. The following promotions occurred last week:

Lieutenants George McKay, L. Davise, S. T. Loomis, George Nesper, and H. U. Spencer were all promoted to Captains. Lieut. Loomis, or more familiarly, the "squire," who is regimental quartermaster, now acting A.Q.M., declined the proffered elevation, preferring his present position to any attitude that would throw him in charge of men. Q. M. Sergent Frank Harmon fills the "squire's" big boots, (No. 14) in his department, without stumbling either. The regiment is now almost bare of Lieutenants and some companies are without a commissioned officer, yet there are sergeants possessing every attribute that make brave, intelligent and efficient officers, who ought to be promoted ... [4]

Some of the more fortunate members of the 7th Ohio were spared the monotony and tribulations of camp life in the early months of 1864. Their local newspapers duly noted their arrivals.

Dr. I. S. King, of Ravenna, of Co. G, 7th O.V.I., has been honorably discharged the service, having served the term of enlistment. He is now at home with his family. [Dr. Ira S. King, hospital steward, was once reported in the newspaper to have been killed in the Battle of Winchester back in May of '62. He was discharged for disability March 15, 1864. [5]]

Lieutenant H. M. Dean, of Co. G, 7th O.V.I., was in town a few hours on Thursday last [March 24th]. He has been on detached duty in Columbus for a month or more. A few cases of Small Pox had occurred in Company A, and two deaths transpired. [Apparently, the Four Horsemen of the Apocalypse never went on furlough. The red horse of War, the white horse of Civil Strife, the black horse of Hunger, and the pale horse of Death kept a close watch over each encampment.] [6]

Lt. Christian W. Nesper, Company H, returned to Cleveland on February 4th. Nesper, who was born in Germany, operated a cigar-making firm in Cleveland.

From The Seventh. – Lieut. Nesper arrived in town yesterday, from the Seventh Ohio. He states that four companies of that noble old regiment have re-enlisted. We should none of us feel like blaming the few remaining soldiers of the Seventh if they should decide that the three years of toil and danger to which they have been exposed had been their share of contribution to the war. But these veterans are tireless and unceasing in their devotion, and while the war lasts, the heroes of the Seventh will be found in the front ranks of the defenders of the Union. [7]

When Lt. Nesper remarked that four companies re-enlisted, it should be remembered that these companies were not even close to the full strength of 100 men each. At one point, Lt. Nesper's Co. H was down to 13 men on duty. Whether these men were mesmerized by the patriotic appeal from their officers or truly believed in the cause of the Union, the truth was known only to them. Perhaps, the inducement of a $402 bounty and a thirty day furlough to go back home to visit their kinfolk and friends carried a more practical weight in the decision to veteranize for three more years. Nevertheless, those who had re-enlisted left Bridgeport for home on March 6th and returned on April 6, 1864. [8]

Many of the men of the 7th Ohio believed that they would be mustered out of the army in late April. Did they have a legitimate complaint or was it simply wishful thinking, a misunderstanding, or a bit of conniving on someone's part? The following letter to the *Cleveland Leader* passionately stated the case of one soldier who believed that the State of Ohio was reneging on a promise for an early mustering out date.

From the Seventh O.V.I.

There seems to be a difficulty in the Seventh of an important character, and one in which the friends of that regiment will feel a deep interest.

We append a statement of the case from a written letter by one of the Seventh. We should like to see the difficulty properly adjusted.

Bridgeport, Ala., March 10, 1864.

Great excitement pervades our camp, and that not without a cause.

On the evening of the 8th inst., an order from the War Department was read on the dress-parade assuring the battle scarred heroes that they would not be mustered out on the 20t^h of April, according to agreement, but held until the 20th of June. They were assured when they enlisted into the three years' service, out of the three months' [service], that their term of service would date from the first enlistment. The order also refers to the recruits in the regiment, and to the astonishment of all, declares that they will be held for the full term of three years. These recruits enlisted about one year and a half ago, with the understanding from the recruiting officer, Captain Cross, and with the assurance from Adjutant-General Hill, of the State of Ohio, that should we enlist for an old regiment in the field, our term of service or enlistment would expire with that of the regiment. We do not begrudge this term of service to our country; no, Heaven forbid! But when we enlisted for the field of strife, we were to be mustered out at the same time and place with the original organization.

But now the War Department holds that there were no *remarks* on the *muster rolls*, stating that we were enlisted with the understanding that our term of service expired with that of the regiment. Now the question is, are we to remain in the field just because of the officer in charge neglected to state on the muster rolls that we were enlisted with the express understanding that when the regiment's term expired ours did also. Has the War Department become so corrupt as to deal so unjustly with us, simply because the recruiting officer failed to do his duty in this respect? We trust not. Then where is the fault? Is it with Adjutant-General Hill of the State? These questions are difficult to answer correctly. We hardly know whether Adjutant-General Hill gave his word that our term of service would expire with that of the regiment on his own responsibility, or not; but this we do know – that everyone intrusted [sic] with such an office as Adjutant-General Hill of a State, should be very careful not to say one thing and at the same time mean something else or the opposite. Surely, the War Department keeps posted in the workings of its *agents*, if not, it ought. If it is the intention of the War Department to hold men three years, and at the same time enlist them with the understanding to serve the unexpired term of an old regiment and then inform them that their term of service would not expire with the old regiment. [The thought of this incomplete sentence continues in the next paragraph.]

Where is the honesty? Surely our Government can get men without enlisting them under false pretenses, and then tell them they are to serve nearly twice as long as the agreement calls for. It is only a polite way of conscripting us. Had we enlisted with the understanding to serve three years, we would serve that time willingly, but when assured that our term of service would expire with that of the regiment, what could we do? Nothing, but place confidence in those in authority over us, and now is that trust to be betrayed? We believe that our government is yet all right, but that some of its agents are not what they ought to be, or else they never would have falsely represented the intentions of the Government. If the War Department gave instructions to enlist men as we were enlisted, surely the intention was to muster us out at the expiration of the term of the regiment.

R. S. [9]

Regardless of the protests of the 7th Ohio, the recruits of the regiment were destined to serve the full term of service. They and the men who had veteranized were to be incorporated into the 5th Ohio when the members of that regiment and the 7th Ohio mustered out in June.

In the meantime, preparations were being made for the spring and summer campaign of 1864. On March 18th, Gen. Sherman assumed command of the Military Division of the Mississippi. Gen. Grant now headed the entire Union Army. Neither of these men were known in the past to idly encamp for long periods of time; they were the type of commanders who liked to get at the enemy. From now on, the objective was to destroy the Confederate armies, and if necessary to wipe out the industrial, agricultural, and financial props of the enemy's forces.

The 11th and 12th Corps were consolidated into the 20th Corps under Gen. Hooker. Gen. John Geary commanded one of the four divisions in the new corps, and the 7th Ohio was still under Geary.

Supplies of all kinds were stockpiled in Chattanooga and Bridgeport. It was a certainty that the big push would soon begin. Some of the men of the western troops had witnessed Shiloh, Vicksburg, Chickamauga, and Chattanooga. Others had seen Antietam, Fredericksburg, Chancellorsville, and Gettysburg when they were in the east. In light of these past battles, there had to be some serious doubts among the original members of the 7th Ohio if they could make it to mid-June without being shot to death, horribly wounded, or victimized by some disease.

On April 12th, the 7th Ohio became part of a picked command under Gen. Geary. The troops embarked on a steamer and two scows at Bridgeport and went on an expedition down the Tennessee River. Sgt. Wilson phrased it as a journey that was made "with a view to recreation and adventure." The Union troops were fired upon by bushwhackers and Confederate pickets along the 110 mile journey. While on the boats, two members of the 7th Ohio were wounded (Pvt. James B. Auxer and Pvt. William H. Poor of Company F), one through the face and the other through the head. For these two men it may have been an adventurous trip, but it could hardly have been recreational. The results of the expedition were 47 enemy boats destroyed, disruption of the Confederate mail service, knowledge of the location and number of enemy pickets, and four captured rebels. The troops were back at Bridgeport by April 16th. [10]

With 39 days remaining in the service for the original members of the 7th Ohio, the regiment and Geary's division began the Union campaign of 1864 on May 3rd when they marched from Bridgeport to Shell Mound. The weather was sultry so Geary moved his men at early dawn on the 4th. They passed through the Wauhatchie Valley and progressed over the narrow and hilly road that led to Rocky Face Ridge. [11]

In the next three days the regiment snaked over and around the rugged terrain which offered scenic views, but also grim reminders of past bloodshed. On May 5th the regiment crossed the Chickamauga battlefield. They arrived at Pea Vine Church on the 6th. On the following day the troops crossed Taylors Ridge, the steep eminence where the regiment was mauled a little over five months previously.

On May 8th, Geary's Division ran into the enemy at Dug's Gap on Rocky Face Ridge. Under the cover of the woods, Lt. Col. McClellan's regiment was ordered into line at 2:00 P.M.

> ...Orders were given to advance directly to the front, which was across open fields until the foot of the ridge was reached, the sides of which were rocky and very steep and covered

with a dense undergrowth of pine shrubs. No opposition was offered to our advance, when, at a temporary halt for rest at about two-thirds the way to the summit, we were removed from our position in the line by the left flank to a ridge or spur from the mountain side commanding the road leading to the summit. We were ordered into line in a position commanding this road and by order of Gen. Geary there remained as a reserve.

On this day the Seventh Ohio was quite fortunate; among the 11 commissioned officers and 228 men who came under fire, there were no casualties. [12]

Sgt. Lawrence Wilson considered the role of the 7th Ohio and Geary's Division as a vigorous diversionary attack while other troops passed through Snake Gap farther down the ridge. Wilson also felt that Gen. Geary deliberately spared the Seventh by placing it in reserve, since that regiment had more than paid its dues at Ringgold. This time it was the 29th Ohio that was mauled by the rebels. [13]

From May 9th through the 11th, Gen. Geary did not spare the Seventh. The regiment was out front doing picket duty. For them, it was a temporary lull as Sherman continued to put pressure on Gen. Joseph Johnston's Confederate Army.

At about 7:00 A.M., Thursday, May 12, the Seventh marched from Mill Creek Gap in a southerly direction and arrived at Snake Creek Gap at sundown, where they bivouacked for the night. At noon on the following day, the troops marched until 5:00 P.M. when it came upon Sherman's outer lines, which were skirmishing with the enemy. For three days the 7th Ohio moved along the line in support positions; however, the situation was far from being calm and restful.

At 4 P.M. on the 14th the regiment moved to the extreme left of the battle line. It was a weary all-day march through fields and woods, up and down steep hillsides. This put them in position for the engagement at Resaca, Georgia on May 15th.

[At] 10 a.m. May 15 ... the regiment was ordered to the right to the support of the Third Division, then heavily engaged in resisting the charge of the enemy. The regiment in line of bat-

The Ohio Monument on Lookout Mt. as seen from the Cravens' House lot. To the left of the picture there is a sharp drop-off, and to the right there is a sharp ascent to the crest. Such terrain confronted Sherman's army on the way to Atlanta in 1864. Photo by Lora Staats.

tle advanced to within a few paces of the crest of the hill, in front of which were two lines of battle, and rested upon the ground. While lying in this position 5 men of my regiment [McClellan's] were struck with the enemy's balls. None were dangerously wounded. After lying here about an hour I was ordered to support the One hundred and forty-seventh Pennsylvania Veteran Volunteers. We moved to the immediate front and formed on the right of that regiment, the regiment being in a ravine. Forty men were sent to the crest of the hill in advance as sharpshooters, their position being protected by piles of rails, breast-works having been built and artillery got into position on a commanding hill a few paces to our rear. At about 10 p.m. the regiment was ordered to join the remainder of the brigade, then lying in a ravine to our right and near the road running east and west. Here arms were stacked and the men laid down to rest. I was aroused at about 11 p.m. by rapid discharges of musketry, and caused the regiment to fall in and be in readiness for any emergency. By order of Gen. Geary three companies of my regiment were deployed on the crest of the hill to stop the retreat of stragglers from the front. The firing soon ceased and the regiment rested undisturbed until daylight. [14]

On May 16th the enemy withdrew and the Union soldiers wasted no time in pursuing them. The 7th Ohio fell in line at 9 A.M., and another full day of action was under way. The regiment headed east and by 5 P.M. they had crossed Connesauga Creek and moved on to Coosawattee Creek. Here the cavalry had located a body of rebels in the woods on the opposite bank. The Seventh was ordered a half mile to the left to support the artillery on some higher ground. After the artillery blasted the woods where the enemy was first spotted, the Union troops were able to cross the creek without opposition. The regiment rejoined the brigade at 9 P.M.; and after crossing the Coosawattee, the Seventh encamped.

The regiment rested until the noon hour on the 17th, and then the men marched eight miles and halted for the night near Calhoun.

The Seventh fell into line at 4 A.M. on the 18th and began a forced march of 15 miles. The fatiguing march was principally across fields and over mountains. After sunset they went into camp.

May 19th saw more of the same hard marching until 4 P.M. when the Union troops ran into the enemy near Cassville. Here the Seventh was put into line of battle on a wooded hillside. The regiment remained at this location until 10 A.M. on the 21st when it withdrew to a wooded area one mile to the rear. On the morning of the 23rd, Geary's Division continued the march south. They passed through Cassville and Cass Station. Around 4 P.M. the 7th Ohio crossed the Etowah River, marched two more miles, and camped for the night. Early the next day, the regiment moved forward, and at sunset they halted for the night on Hickory Ridge. Thus far, "Uncle Billy" Sherman had expended a lot of shoe leather with his flanking marches; and although he continued to press the rebel army, he did not expend his soldiers' lives in massive frontal assaults up to this point.

May 25th loomed as another long and energy-sapping day as the men plodded through more dense woods and up steep ridges. It was made more difficult by the intense cold and a severe pelting rain that fell throughout this spring day. The Seventh was in the advance when they ran into hot resistance from the rebels. Some of the boys would not be able to answer the muster-out, which was about three weeks away. Lt. Col. McClellan described the events of the day.

> May 25, received orders to take the advance of the brigade, which had the advance of the division and entire column; moved off at 7a.m. At about a mile from camp, by order of Gen. Geary, I deployed seven companies as skirmishers, three on the right and four on the left of the road. Owing to the density of the underbrush and rank growth of weeds, which were wet with rain, the advance of the skirmishers was very slow and toilsome. At about three miles from the previous night's camp, and when approaching Pumpkin Vine Creek, our advance was fired upon by the enemy's pickets, who were stationed at the bridge; the extreme right of my skirmishers was also fired upon by cavalry pickets from the opposite bank of the creek. The enemy had made an attempt to destroy the bridge by tearing up the planking and setting it on fire in several places. With some delay my command crossed and advanced to the hill on the opposite bank. After resting half an hour they again moved forward. Generals Hooker and Geary, with their staffs and

body guards, were well up with, and at times in advance of, the skirmish line. At about 10 a.m., when about two miles beyond the creek, some of General Hooker's body guard, then in advance, were fired upon by the enemy. General Geary immediately ordered me to deploy my reserve to the right and left of the road and move forward on the enemy to relieve General Hooker's body guard, then being driven back. I did so, deploying my three remaining companies, consisting of about sixty-five men, who immediately engaged the enemy and held them at bay until the other regiments of the brigade were advanced in line of battle, pushing the enemy before them something like a mile. During this skirmish I had 1 man killed and 8 wounded. Here we were ordered to remain and throw up breast-works, which was done very hastily. At about 6 p.m., my command was ordered into line, the Fifth Ohio Volunteers on my right and Twenty-ninth Ohio Volunteers on my left, and advanced to the support of the Second and Third Brigades. On getting within range of the enemy's fire while advancing, 3 men were killed and 15 were wounded. One shell from the enemy's guns exploded in the ranks, killing two men and wounding six others. My command lay in position in the front line until 11 o'clock on the 26th instant, ...[15]

From May 26th to the 31st the Seventh Ohio spent most of the time on the front lines. The skirmishers, who were placed fifty yards in front of the breastworks, were continually under fire and returning the favor. The enemy also opened up with artillery fire. In all of this, just one man of the Seventh was wounded; he was hit in the face by a musket ball.

At last, the final month of service arrived for the 7th Ohio. On June 1st the regiment was withdrawn from the lines and moved to the left and rear of the Union position. On the 2nd, they moved further to the left in the direction of Allatoona Church. Heavy storms of driving rain, gusty winds, and pelting hail made the move more physically demanding.

From June 3-5, the regiment remained in position behind the 23rd Corps. For those who had thoughts of soon returning home, some serious questions raced through their minds. Would the Ohio boys have to serve their last 20 days, or would they be granted the miracle of an early departure from the service? Would they be able to stay out of harm's way?

On June 6th, Johnston's Confederate Army evacuated their works, so Geary's Division and the Union Army moved forward. Fortunately for the Seventh, they occupied a position behind the breastworks from June 7-11.

The 11th of June loomed as another spring day to be endured behind the Union breastworks. However, at nine o'clock in the morning, Lt. Col. Samuel McClellan's eyes welled with tears as he read the order that had just arrived. The Seventh Ohio was immediately relieved from the service, and the recruits and veterans were to report to the 5th Ohio. Since it would not be proper for an emotional Lieutenant Colonel to pass along the lines with the glad tidings, McClellan sent Sgt. Major Newton K. Hubbard to deliver the news to the men.[16]

At the announcement of the order to the men, an outburst of exultation rent the air. Gleeful shouts, handshaking, back-slapping, and caps thrown into the air marked the jubilant scene. Then the soldiers of the Seventh became strangely subdued when it was realized that the recruits and their veteranized friends had to stay behind.

On that June morning, the Seventh formed into two lines; those who were going home were on one side, and across from them were the men who were to continue to wage war. As the original members of the Seventh marched to the rear, sobs and tears were in evidence in both lines. The occasion marked the termination, hopefully only temporarily, of human bonds that were strengthened in common suffering and forged in battle, bonds that were stronger than those of brotherhood. It also marked the end of the 7th Ohio Volunteer Infantry as a fighting force.

In his report of September 15, Gen. John Geary especially mentioned the 7th Ohio.

> On the 11th [of June], the term of service of the Seventh Ohio Volunteers, Lieutenant-Colonel McClellan, having expired, the regiment departed for the North. During its long connection with my division,

this regiment, by gallant service upon many fields, on which it lost heavily, earned for itself a reputation of which Ohio may well be proud. [17]

The long journey home for the 7th Ohio began with a march to Big Shanty Station. The next part of the odyssey was by train. The regiment arrived in Chattanooga on the night of June 15th. The departure to Nashville was on the 17th, and the train arrived there at 6 P.M. on the 18th.

The 7th boarded a steamer at Nashville on the 19th, but their patience was tested a little more because the steamer did not leave until 4 A.M. on the 20th. The returning soldiers were still not completely out of harm's way. Bushwhackers were still a deadly menace on the Cumberland River, and two soldiers of the regiment were wounded as the boat steamed toward the Ohio River.

Meanwhile in the Western Reserve, there were those who were anxiously awaiting the return of the Seventh. The *Portage County Democrat* printed the following item.

Return of the 7th Ohio.

The Cincinnati Commercial of the 24th says; –

7th Ohio, Lieutenant Colonel Samuel McClellan commanding, will arrive in this city to-day, enroute home, to be mustered out. They come direct from the front of Sherman's army, and left Nashville on the steamer Mercury. The regiment numbers now about 250 men. It was raised principally on the Reserve and has made a brilliant record in the past three years. [18]

The regiment landed at Cincinnati at 3 A.M. on June 25th. The Queen City was prepared to fete the 7th and 5th Ohio Regiments with welcoming speeches and a grand feast, but for one of the soldiers of the 7th Ohio, tragedy was lurking in the Ohio River.

Sgt. Oliver Trembley of Company C was one of the first volunteers who patriotically answered Mr. Lincoln's original call for troops. Trembley entered the three months' service on April 25, 1861. On June 20th of 1861, he enlisted for three years. The sergeant was extremely lucky to have escaped three years of service in some mighty hot spots without receiving even a flesh wound; but on June 24, 1864 his luck ran out.

A Very Sad Event.

The drowning of Sergeant O. C. Trembley, of the gallant 7th, while on the Ohio River, is a very touching event.

The brave Trembley had fought in twenty-eight battles, had his gun shot from his hands several times, had bullets put through his clothes, and yet, was never wounded. After serving more than three years, he was returning home to his friends. But twenty-one years of age, life was yet before him with all its joyous anticipations. In a few more hours, he was to receive the kisses and embraces of father, mother, sister and brother. To die after having endured all this, was truly sorrowful.

Every effort was made for his recovery, but as he was unable to swim, he was immediately strangled on falling into the water.

An event so peculiarly sad, must bring tears of sympathy for the afflicted friends, from many eyes. [19]

The newspapers on the Western Reserve hailed the return of the Seventh Ohio. The unbounded enthusiasm matched or surpassed that of when the citizens bade them adieu back in the spring of 1861. Lost in the celebration was the fact that the Seventh's recruits and veteranized men were still slugging it out in Sherman's Atlanta Campaign.

Turn Out to Receive the Seventh.

The citizens of Cleveland need but to be informed of the arrival of the glorious Seventh to turn out en masse and give them a welcome. It is impossible, at this moment, to say just when they will arrive, but it will be within a day or two. Let no one refrain from hanging out his banner, and cheering lustily and well when this remnant of the brave *fourteen hundred* march through our streets. Every one who has a flag should wave it. Every one who has a handkerchief or a hat should swing it. Every one who has a voice should shout. [20]

"The news had gone the rounds on Saturday night that the regiment would arrive on Sunday morning, and, therefore, when with the early morning, the fire bells rang a loud alarm, all understood the signal. At half after seven the bells commenced their clangor, and, simultaneously, streams of people, from every quarter, began pouring their floods towards the Union Depot, where the regiment was expected to debark. A crowd which was numbered by its thousands had already assembled when the whistle for an approaching train on the Columbus road announced that the "bully Seventh" – the pride and glory of the Reserve – was coming. As the train rapidly approached, the scanty number of its cars suggested a sad and painful contrast with the full train which bore the gallant regiment away. But the time for mournful reflection was but short. The shrill whistle of the engine – the thunder of the nearing train – the shrieking of the tortured brakes – the gradual stopping of the approaching train – and the boys, their journey done, their three years work complete, are grasping by the hand and folding in their arms the friends and loved ones from whom they have been so long separated.

… An hour slipped by unnoticed, in such individual greetings, while the boys, having debarked and stacked arms, exchanged welcomes with their friends. By this time the crowd had swelled to thousands, the cannon had ceased their thunderous welcome, the company of discharged members of the Seventh, 45 strong, under command of Captain A. A. Cavanah, and headed by the "Temperance Band' had reached the depot, and the breakfast, which the provident Military Committee had arranged for the boys, was in readiness.

The regiment, therefore, under the command of Lieutenant Colonel McClellan, filed around to where the ample tables were spread, and took their seats. Here a substantial breakfast, consisting of coffee, softbread, meat, &c., 'topping off' with strawberries, was provided them, which the boys seemed to enjoy excellently...

After the meal was over, the regiment resumed its arms, leaving its baggage to be carried by wagons, and took up its march to the Square. Its line of march was an ovation. Everywhere the streets were lined with spectators, the pavements overflowed, the windows were filled, the doors and balconies and roofs were crowded, flags hung from roofs and from ropes stretched across the street, and shout on shout greeted the advancing column. First, after the police force, came the old members of the Seventh bearing the second flag which had floated over its columns – for the first is now among the treasured relics of the war in the State House at Columbus. Then the regiment itself, bearing their third flag, keeping admirable time and order, and, even with its scattered and wasted ranks, looking fit to withstand an avalanche. And then – saddest and most touching of all – the invalid soldiers of the regiment, looking out, with an interest that sickness and wounds could not subdue, upon the scene.

So greeted everywhere with cheers, in which all joined, none feeling that the Sabbath was profaned by this general welcome, the regiment swept up Water Street, up Superior, around the Square, and to the United States building, where thousands were already gathered in anticipation of its coming. Here, under the shade of the building, Colonel McClellan formed his men in a square, and, soon as the vast crowd had been reduced to quiet, they were addressed by J. C. Grannis, Esq., City Attorney, on behalf of the city of Cleveland ... [Gov. John Brough then addressed the regiment and welcomed them on behalf of the State of Ohio.]

When the Governor had closed, the regiment gave three loud and ringing cheers for him, followed by three times three cheers for the City of Cleveland and its cordial welcome to the regiment. These were responded to by three as hearty and thunderous cheers as were ever given, for the glorious and gallant Seventh Ohio...

The reception was over for the day, and the regiment filed away toward Camp Cleveland, escorted by Captain Cavanah's company consisting of the old members of the Seventh and followed by a throng of thousands. They were comfortably quartered yesterday at Camp Cleveland, where they are now the only troops, and where they are comfortably settled. It will probably be several days before their papers are completed and they are mustered out of service. Meantime, they will probably all be furloughed for a day or two, to visit their homes. We understand that the Painesville Company (Company D) will receive a grand ovation at Painesville to-day, and that Superintendent Nottingham has granted a free pass to the company to Painesville and return..."[21]

Some of the original Franklin Rifles and Tyler Guards were seen on furlough in Portage County.

RETURN OF THE 7TH OHIO. – The glorious and brave 7th have come home. The regiment reached Cleveland on Sunday morning and were received by a most enthusiastic public demonstration, Gov. Brough was one of the speakers.

The Regiment left the front on the 11th of June and arrived at Cincinnati on Saturday morning, and in company with the 5th Ohio had a most magnificent reception at Mozart Hall.

Upon Monday, July 4th, a grand Western Reserve picnic is to be given the 7th Ohio, at Cleveland in honor of their return from the fields which they have nobly invested with honor and glory and with blood. Let every one attend who can, that the occasion may be worthy of the deeds done by our brave sons.

Upon Monday a few of the Portage County members reached Ravenna to greet their friends and families. The following is as complete as it was possible to procure on Monday:

Company G – Capt. Braden of Warren, formerly of Co. H, commanding. Sergeant Lazarus, Deerfield. Sergeant Furry, Streetsboro. Corporal L. Reed, Ravenna. Corporal May, Atwater. Drum Major R. W. Orvis, Edinburg. J. McFarland, Charlestown. J. Bacon, Palmyra. J. Potts, Wm. Wise, Suffield. Wm. Ripple, Atwater. V. Reynolds, Henry O. Barber, Lyman Beery, Ravenna. H. Owen, Benton, Stacey Shaw. [sic]

Company F – Wm. Perry, Nelson. A. Nicholson, Franklin. Sergeant Eli Northrop, Edinburgh. M. V. Burt, Brimfield.

The regiment is not yet mustered out, but probably will be in the course of the week.

Gov. Brough in the course of his remarks said to the Regiment:

"I will not read your record – it would take too long. My memory would not serve me to tell the fields of slaughter and death on which you have won renown. Standing, as I do, in the position of father to all the regiments of the State, I cannot discriminate between my children. But without disparagement I can say that no regiment has returned or remains to come after you, bearing a more perfect record than the Seventh Ohio. [Cheers.] You have crowned us with honor, as well as yourselves." [22]

On Sunday, July 3rd, those members of the regiment who were still in camp at Cleveland Heights marched to Erie Cemetery. The remains of Colonels Creighton and Crane were taken from a vault and escorted by the 7th to another vault at Woodland Cemetery. [23]

The Pic Nic to the Seventh Regiment.

Cleveland, July 7, 1864.

Editor Leader: Having seen no notice of the impromptu pic nic of yesterday in this morning's issue, I have taken upon myself the duty of reporter.

At two o'clock P.M., several ladies met on the ground attached to the "Oak Grove House," on the Brooklyn Road, a delightful spot, and proceeded to arrange a tempting dinner for the remaining members of the Seventh Ohio Regiment. Baskets, dishes, lemons, tubs, ice, and all accessries [sic] to a modest banquet were there in profusion. While this was going on a ring was formed and a gay party engaged in a merry game. Judging from the zest with which the veterans entered into it, one would suppose they had been banished from social amusements for three times three years.

After the repast, Surgeon Bellows made an appropriate little speech, one that could be heard without straining the neck, and being half smothered in a "Fourth of July crowd." The scene and the occasion were really more touching than a public demonstration could be.

The Surgeon told the men he thought some of them would re-enlist before long. No doubt they will, for after all, there is a fascination about the smell of powder, to say nothing of the jolly evenings around the campfire, and the pleasant acquaintances formed. Will it not be rather difficult for some of them to separate and take up the work that was laid aside when the call sounded from Camp Taylor, three years ago? There is something like the commencement day at College in the disbanding of the regiment. The soldiers are the graduate class.

At any rate they will not forget that one of their ovations was arranged entirely by the ladies; that it was held in Cleveland, July 6, 1864, and that it was a most hearty affair.

"BUSYBODY." [24]

Seven companies mustered out on July 6th, and the last three companies left the service on the following day. All of the men had to wait until the 8th to receive their pay. Sgt. Wilson recalled the day of July 8th as one of joy in being free from military rule and discipline, yet there was a "peculiar sadness" in saying farewell to their comrades. [25]

Chapter Eight

"So teach us to number our days"

It had been thirty-eight and a half months since the Franklin Rifles (Company F) volunteered in the fever-pitched, patriotic atmosphere that immediately followed the firing upon Fort Sumter in South Carolina. Now, in July of 1864, only *nine* men were coming home to Portage County after mustering out at Cleveland. Four other men of the company came home after mustering out at convalescent centers. Seventeen men of the Franklin Rifles had veteranized, and one of them had already perished near Dallas, Georgia on May 25th. In a short time, one of the returnees would re-enter the service.

The first men of the Tyler Guards (Company G) had left Ravenna on April 24, 1861. In a boisterous, holiday mood the seventeen men were escorted to the railroad depot by a blaring military band and an artillery company; and all were preceded by the school children carrying a banner. With additional eager volunteers, the ranks of the Tyler Guards quickly filled to a regulation-sized company of 100 men. Now, twenty-eight men of the company came home on the train to Ravenna. Another man was mustered out from a convalescent center. Two of the returnees would soon re-enlist. Only four men of the Tyler Guards had veteranized.

When the original members of the Franklin Rifles and the Tyler Guards left Portage County to preserve the Union, there was quite a fanfare in the local newspapers; but such was not the case when they returned home in July of 1864. The Union was still in dire straits, and stories of tremendous slaughter and peril commanded the attention of the editors. Thousands of Union soldiers were being killed and wounded since Gen. Grant began his southern move on May 4th. While the men of the Seventh were mustering out on July 7th, the Union Army was stymied at Petersburg, Virginia. Gen. Jubal Early's Confederate troops were moving north out of the Shenandoah Valley, destroying and burning property, extorting large sums of money from property owners, and threatening to do the same to the federal capital. In the West, Sherman's army was approaching Atlanta with growing casualties. The war went on.

Yet, the Seventh Ohio had paid its dues; and some of the regiment's men were still fighting with Sherman. In time, the latter would see the fall of Atlanta, participate in the March to the Sea, receive Gen. Johnston's surrender, and march through Washington, D.C. in the Grand Review on May 24, 1865.

In the final analysis, 1,365 men had enrolled in the Seventh Ohio. The number killed in battle was 184. Another 498 were wounded. Eighty-nine men died from disease. In Company F one officer and 13 men were killed; Company G suffered 19 killed. Nine men of Company F died from disease or accidents; Company G lost one officer and nine men due to disease or accident. Such were the cold statistics. [1]

Walter Dickinson of Randolph in Portage County remarked on the expectations and fears regarding the men of several regiments that returned to his township.

> ...Fears had been expressed that when the war closed the country would be overrun with idlers who had lost all interest in labor. It had been said that those who had served in the war would be disposed to remain in the Sunny South. But one individual from town remained [down South], and he was in the service of the United States Government. Those who lived through to the end of the war, with the exception of a few transient persons, returned and went to work. Some had saved a sufficient amount to buy farms or to set themselves in business. [26]

Dickinson gave the impression that the veterans, at least those with an industrious nature, returned home to live happily ever after. Surely, the transition from the life of a front-line soldier to a productive citizen must have been a trying experience for many veterans of the 7th Ohio and other front-lone troops. These were not the same young men who cheerfully and enthusiastically volunteered to save the Union in 1861 – a time when their friends, sweethearts, and neighbors hurrahed and waved handkerchiefs and flags as the train chugged out of sight. Coming home were men whose bodies and minds were forever altered.

These were men whose senses were stimulated to the extremes and often beyond. Their eyes had seen human bodies that were mangled and dismembered in every conceivable way. They had witnessed the convulsions of their dying friends. On the larger battlefields the carnage of wrecked bodies could be seen for mile after mile. Flies and maggots feasted on the exposed flesh and filled every orifice of the rapidly decaying corpses. The survivors' nostrils and lungs were filled with the unforgettable stench of the rotten and bloated men, horses, and mules. They had felt the concussion of bursting shells. Their eardrums were assaulted by the roaring explosions, the hail storm of zipping musket balls, the shrieks and screams of their terrified, wounded and dying comrades. They had felt the stickiness of warm blood spattered all over them, some of it perhaps their own, some of it the blood and brains from a nearby fellow soldier. Some of them could recall the horrendous smacks and thuds of bashing in the skull of a foe with the butt-end of a musket. Their skin and extremities had been assailed by the winter winds and snow, freezing rain and hail; and they had been subjected to sunburn and heatstroke on the searing hot, humid summer days as they were force-marched in their woolen uniforms through clouds of suffocating dust to an impending battle. Swarming mosquitoes, gnats, ticks, and other biting insects sucked their blood. Periods of inadequate, wormy food, and stagnant, putrid drinking water had ruined many a digestive track for a lifetime. On many occasions they had been deprived of sleep for days on end, not only by the combat and elements around them, but also by their own intense fears. They had undergone agonies inflicted by a determined enemy, but they also knew in their heart of hearts that they had done inhuman deeds and inflicted agony on other human beings.

The stress of combat and the fear was so excruciating that there were reports of men with self-inflicted wounds who hoped to escape the next brutal confrontation with death. Some men even committed suicide rather than face another day of this miserable existence. During the Civil War the terms "battle fatigue" and "post-traumatic stress syndrome" were unknown, but the conditions were present. They were often described as "nostalgia," which is defined as follows:

> Nostalgia is a cluster of symptoms marked by excessive physical fatigue, an inability to concentrate, an unwillingness

to eat or drink leading at times to anorexia, a feeling of isolation and total frustration in a military environment ... Tragically, nostalgia in itself was often fatal, especially if the soldier's emotional resistance was weakened by a wound. [3]

Civil War army nurses experienced the same traumatic conditions as the fighting men. The stories of 98 women nurses are told in *Our Army Nurses*. Most of these women had to leave the service due to poor health caused by long hours of work and disease. They suffered mental stress brought on by witnessing the suffering of their patients, the futility in trying to save many of their lives, and attending many sorrowful, heart-wrenching deathbed scenes. A few of the women died while in the service of their country. Two of the women nurses came from the area of the Franklin Rifles and the Tyler Guards. Matilda Morris hailed from Randolph, and Eunice Brown lived in Windham of Portage County. [4]

According to Gerald F. Lindeman, some of the soldiers became "hardened" or "coarsened" to the carnage around them. They would employ gallows humor, play practical jokes on their more concerned brethren, and look upon the inhumanity in a dispassionate manner. One combatant remarked: "Men can get accustomed to everything; and the daily sight of blood and mangled bodies so blunted their finer sensibilities as almost to blot out all love, all sympathy from the heart, and to bring into prominence the baser qualities of man, selfishness, greed, and revenge." [5]

Other soldiers reacted to their experiences by becoming depressed by the disappearance of the regiment, their officers, and friends. Such was the case for the dispirited 7th Ohio, which lost so many officers and men at Ringgold, Georgia. Soldiers began to despair that their chances of survival were nil. A soldier of the 8th Infantry, who was in the same situation as the 7th Ohio, remarked: "Nearly everyone I know has been killed or wounded, and if this campaign (Sherman's Georgia campaign) with its senseless assaults of entrenched positions and its ceaseless tributes of blood and death, is to continue much longer, my turn is sure to come soon, and I want to avoid that if I can honorably do so." [6]

The mental images and physical sensations related to the gruesome events in which the combatants participated were reviewed even in their sleep. James M. McPherson cited one Confederate soldier: "Many soldiers fought battles over in nightmares, which 'frighten me more than ever the fight did when I was wide awake.' "[7] It is reasonable to assume that these nightmares occurred to some degree in all of the soldiers who had experienced the shock of combat. In later years following the Civil War, it is quite conceivable that the survivors of the Seventh Ohio and other regiments tossed violently in their sleep, unconsciously yelled or groaned in the darkness, and then bolted upright in a clammy sweat as scenes of buzzing bullets, exploding shells, the faces of the dead, shouts and screams, and their own near-death experiences flashed across their minds and haunted them.

Now, the veterans of the 7th Ohio Infantry were required to re-enter the "polite" society of civilian life in their towns or on the farms of Portage County and northeast Ohio. Camp talk and three years of army slang had to be cleaned up. As Gerald F. Lindeman expertly phrased it, "Killing once again became homicide, foraging was once again theft, and incendiarism arson." [8]

One saving grace for the Civil War veteran was that the public generally accepted and even lauded the deeds that he had done. The Union was saved, and a valuable service had been performed. Such public support was denied some future American veterans.

If the 7th Ohio was to make the successful transition to civilian life – getting back to work, buying that little farm, or starting up his own business as Walter Johnson viewed it – the veteran would have to suppress his painful memories of the war. To do so was to protect his self-image and how others perceived him. To admit of bad dreams and other uncontrollable effects of combat might insinuate insanity in those pre-psychiatry days. To boast, or even converse, about his role in the inhumanity of combat or of his stark fear and terror was out of the question. The fact that he had been a killer, a thief, and an arsonist were not self-images that he wanted for himself, nor what he wanted his neighbors to think of him. To exhibit even a trace of whining or complaining would be unmanly and unpatriotic to *him*.

Yet, no matter how much the veterans tried to suppress their painful memories of the war, for many of them there were daily reminders. The effects of dysentery and other health problems lingered for years. The number of wounded in the 7th Ohio totaled 498, or 36.5 % of the regiment.[9] The wounds could ache and fester for a lifetime. The veterans who had limbs amputated were by their own appearance reminders of the horrors of the Civil War and the pain that it inflicted. Advertisements in the post-war newspapers illustrate that the sale of the latest variety of prosthetic devices was a booming business in the Portage County area. With the unrestricted use of opiates and alcoholic potions, which was common for the time, the veteran's pain reliever could become his curse of drug dependency and alcoholism. In spite of the dangers of these products, the newspaper advertisements indicate that the sale of these elixirs and potions was also a booming business.

There was one segment of the population to whom the veteran could turn, and that was his own kind. He had experienced a "touch of the elbow" from one end of the regiment to the other, whether it was in drill or in line of battle. He had stood "shoulder touching shoulder, forming an unbroken chain across the contested and deadly field." This bond of togetherness extended to every Federal soldier. The veteran of the 7th Ohio could feel that he had served elbow to elbow with other Union soldiers in a nationwide chain. [10]

The Grand Army of the Republic, the G.A.R., held the promise of being a haven for the returned veteran. Not all of the war's experiences had been devastating; there were also good memories and days of camaraderie to share. In addition, the objectives of the G.A.R. appeared to be noble and worthy. First, there was *Fraternity*: "To preserve and strengthen those kind and fraternal feelings which bind together...and perpetuate the memory and history of the dead." The second objective was *Charity*: To assist former comrades as need help and protection and to extend aid to orphans and widows of those who have fallen. The third objective was *Loyalty*: "To maintain true allegiance to the U.S.A.... and to encourage the spread of universal liberty, equal rights, and justice to all men." [11] Eventually, the G.A.R. served as a powerful lobby for soldiers' pensions.

Although the G.A.R. intended to eschew politics, the organization of veterans was ripe pickings as a voting bloc. This political wrangling alienated many veterans. A second detraction of the G.A.R. may have been the elaborate and secretive aspects of the ritual. Nevertheless, the G.A.R. answered the needs of some of the veterans, although some chose to shun the organization.

For the veteran who possessed a political bent, there were ample opportunities to exercise their political passions. One of those events for the "Boys in Blue" of Portage County was the Soldiers and Sailors Convention held at Ravenna on September 22, 1866. It was a call for political action against President Andrew Johnson's reconstruction policies. With much flag-waving and the exploitation of the fear that all of the sacrifice and suffering of the Union soldiers might have been in vain, the response was quite enthusiastic. The editor of the *Portage County Democrat* fanned the fires of discontent over Johnson's "Policy."

> A convention of the Soldiers and Sailors of Portage County, who *do not* endorse "My Policy" of recent date, and the action of the "Philadelphia Convention" of August 14, 1866, but believe that the immense expenditure of life and treasure and their great sacrifices in the Rebellion should not be in vain; who still believe that "treason is the blackest of crimes" and that "in the work of reconstruction, the rebels and traitors should take back seats," and who desire to see the Union established on the basis of the proposed Constitutional Amendment, will meet in the Town Hall at Ravenna, Ohio...
> A full attendance from every township is desired.
> The perils of the hour demand "That you *give another day for your country.*" [Then followed a list with the names of every surviving veteran in the county.] [12]

On the appointed day of the meeting, a large crowd of veterans and other onlookers descended on Citizens Hall. "The Ravenna Silver Cornet Band was engaged for the day and invested the occasion with a pleasant air of martial vigor." It was reminiscent of the scenes at that popular gathering place at the outbreak of the Rebellion.

> "The convention assembled at 11 A.M. and was called to order by Andrew Jackson of the 104th O.V.I. who nominated Gen. Wm. Stedman for President [of the convention]. Gen. Stedman took the stand amid the cheers of the assembly, and addressed his fellow soldiers for about ten minutes, stating the objective for which the convention was called, the purpose of the Pittsburg Convention of the 25th and the duty of all patriotic union men, not the least of whom are

the "Boys in Blue," who after the smoke of the battle and the conflict of arms, are again in their places, as citizens, but who will ever hold the integrity of the Republic and the perpetuity of the Union in the highest reverence and honor."

Other officers for the Ravenna Convention were chosen. Serving on the Committee of Resolutions was a familiar veteran to the 7th Ohio and Company G – Capt. S. S. Reed from Rootstown. Delegates were then elected from each township for the grand convention to be held in Pittsburgh. [13]

> One of the greatest assemblages, if not the greatest ever held in this country, convened in Pittsburg last week composed of the brave Soldiers and Sailors who successfully fought the battles of the Republic, and crushed the bloody rebellion. The surviving braves who presented a living breastwork to the foe, and interposed a barrier of safety between Northern homes, and the bloody minded, barbarian hordes of rebeldom, were out in immense numbers to commune together to perpetuate what their valor had saved...
>
> The Convention was organized on Tuesday noon – the immense concourse being numbered by tens of thousands upon tens of thousands reported. Among the celebrities present were Generals Butler, Banks, Garfield, Schenck, Cochrane, Logan, Hawkins, Barlow, Negley, Shaler, Coggswell, and large numbers of others. A great number of "empty sleeves" were there, which told eloquently and touchingly of the devotion and sufferings of our brave defenders...
>
> A procession, far from embodying all present, was two hours passing a given point. An informant tells us that ten thousand withdrawn from the throng could scarcely have been missed so great was the immense gathering.
>
> With speech and song, and conference by day, and torch-light processions and illuminations by night, the golden hours passed away. The entire city fluttered with flags, and blazed with illuminations. If the base usurper who now sits defiantly in the White House, threatening us with another civil war, to carry devastation through the north, attempts his threatened vengeance, an army will spring to the rescue and meet him at the threshold and overwhelm him and his equally

base and desperate advisors, with condign retribution. Heaven save us from another bloody conflict. [14]

As the presidential election approached in 1868, the votes of the veterans were courted more than ever on the local level. The G.A.R. Post of Randolph actively engaged in politics, especially the promotion of Gen. Grant for the presidency.

> **Soldiers' Reunion.** [We give] a report of the first annual reunion of the soldiers of Randolph, under the auspices of the Grand Army of the republic, Randolph Post, No. 151. The Post comprises only a portion of Randolph's Boys in Blue, but all such, with citizens generally were invited to meet at the Town Hall, on Tuesday evening, last week. So on that evening there was a large assembly of "fair women and brave men" in response to the invitation ... The exercises were opened by singing a number of familiar and favorite army songs, "The Star Spangled Banner," "Battle Cry of Freedom," "Red, White and Blue," &c. This patriotic and inspiring opening of the evening placed everyone in the happiest humor for its enjoyment, and again and again the patriotic choruses reverberated through the hall. The next item of interest was the presentation of a beautiful silk Flag, to the members of the Post by the Ladies of Randolph...

The remainder of the evening was spent in listening to entertainment by an "excellent" string band and "charming" ballads by a female soloist, "feasting on Randolph's ever generous larder," and making patriotic resolutions. What appeared to be the chief aim of the reunion was manifested just prior to the conclusion of the meeting and the singing of the Doxology: "...by a rising vote, every person in the house declared a preference for General Grant for President." [15]

The 7th Ohio Volunteer Infantry began its own reunions on September 10, 1866. Gen. E. B. Tyler, the regiment's first Colonel, traveled from his home in Baltimore, Maryland to attend the re- union in Cleveland.

> Gen. Tyler, on being conducted to the chair, says the *Leader*, made a thrilling and touching address reviewing the

incidents and scenes in which this noble regiment played a conspicuous part, and feelingly referred to the honored dead of the regiment, Colonels Creighton and Crane, and the fallen braves of their command. His speech was listened to with marked attention. At its close the members of the regiment arose simultaneously and gave "three cheers and a tiger" for General Tyler and "three times three" for the Seventh Regiment...[16]

Unlike the Soldiers and Sailors Conventions, local soldier gatherings, and other regimental reunions, the reunions of the 7th Ohio were not politicized. Perhaps the chief reason for this was that the surviving leaders of the regiment were not Radical Republicans. Tyler had been a Democrat before the war. Consequently, there were no resolutions to endorse a particular candidate or certain policy to save the Union through political means. The resolutions at the 1866 reunion, like those of the later reunions, were primarily thankful and businesslike in nature.

Whereas, in the good Providence of God, we, formerly members of the Seventh Ohio Volunteer Infantry, have been preserved from the dangers of war and the sickness of the camp during the suppression of the late terrible rebellion, and have been permitted to meet again in convention: therefore,

Resolved, That we give hearty thanks to Almighty God for the many mercies of the past; and that we tender our heartiest sympathies to the kinsmen and friends of noble officers and men who laid down their lives, and also to our brethren who in body and limb are still suffering from their wounds and sickness.

Resolved, That we unite in a society to be called "The Society of the Survivors of the Seventh Regiment O.V.I."

[The next two resolutions established the offices and future meeting dates for the reunions.]

Resolved, That as speedily as possible, we proceed to procure a suitable lot in the Woodland Cemetery, Cleveland, O., and erect thereon a monument to the memory of our heroic dead; and also that any money remaining in the hands of the Treasurer after defraying the expenses of erecting the monument, shall be distributed among the widows and orphans of the dead, and among the maimed and wounded members of the Seventh. [17]

One would expect the attendance at the reunions of the Seventh to have been substantial, but such was not the case. Only 18 Portage County "boys" attended the 1866 reunion. Five were from Co. F; nine were from Co. G; and four were from other companies in the regiment. Of the 1,092 survivors who had served in the 7th Ohio, around seventy attended the second reunion in 1867. This represented only 6.4 % of the surviving members.

Several reasons could be attributed to the low attendance of the 7th Ohio. First, in the opening resolution of the 1866 reunion there was mention of members who were still suffering from wounds and sickness. Second, the regiment was split in June of 1864 when the three years' men returned home, and the recruits and re-enlisted men went to the 5th Ohio. This may have caused some ill feelings toward the old regiment and a new allegiance to the 5th Ohio. Third, some situations probably left a lasting bitterness. For example, Maj. F. A. Seymour's name never appeared on the list of officers in attendance, and there is no evidence in the local newspapers that he ever attended. Fourth, it is possible that a few veterans could not afford the train fare or the expenses of an overnight trip. Fifth, it is quite likely that many of the 7th Ohio were still suffering from the demoralized state following the battle at Ringgold, where they lost so many officers and men. Earl J. Hess uses the term "Lost Soldiers" for such men. These were men who refused to attend reunions. They felt empty and embittered by their experiences; they had no sense of personal accomplishment; and they saw no redeeming consequences for the war. [18]

Perhaps due in part to the low attendance at reunions, the 7th Ohio and the 29th Ohio held a combined reunion at Painesville on August 8, 1870. The date was chosen in memory of the Battle of Cedar Mountain in which both regiments fought. (Other battles that the regiments had in common were the Shenandoah campaign of 1862, Chancellorsville, Gettysburg, and the campaign in northern Georgia.) "The regiments marched through a number of the streets of the city, led by bands of music. An ox, weighing 500 pounds when dressed, was roasted for the occasion...After the exercises were through with [sic] everyone spent the afternoon according to his own desire, the order being a general shaking of hands all around. In the evening the members of the regiments had a grand ball and supper at the Stockwell House." [19]

One of the grandest 7th Ohio reunions gathered at Ravenna in 1868. The city, and especially the editor of the *Democrat*, considered the occasion one of civic pride and an honor to be the host for the 7th Ohio's reunion.

"HONOR TO THE BRAVE!"
Reunion of the Seventh Ohio
AT RAVENNA, MAY 1ST, 1868.
Splendid ovation to the Boys in Blue.

Friday, May 1st, 1868, the anniversary of the battle of Chancellorsville, was well chosen for the third annual reunion of the gallant 7th Ohio Regiment. In designating Ravenna as the place for the meeting it seems that a most fitting locality was chosen, for nearly all citizens manifested a personal interest in the matter and the local committee of arrangements found the heartiest co-operation. At an early morning hour a large number of flags were displayed upon Main Street, and the beautiful day was devoted to the generous fete. The headquarters of the festival was located at Citizens Hall, the lower room being assigned for the dinner and the upper hall prepared for the meeting of the members of the regiment. At 8 A.M. Gen. E. B. Tyler with others of the 7th arrived upon a train on the C. & P. R.R., and were escorted by the Cornet Band and a delegation of Citizens to the Gillette House. Upon the arrival of the ten o'clock train from Cleveland a large detachment of veterans arrived, who were greeted with a military salute and escorted to the Gillette House by the Band and citizens, as a number of the guests of the day were accompanied by ladies. At eleven A.M., a procession was formed and marched from the Gillette House to Citizens Hall, the Band playing "Hail to the Chief" and other patriotic airs. Arriving at the Hall, a business meeting was called to order by Col. McClellan of Youngstown, President of the 7th regiment Association. The exercises were opened by prayer by Rev. J. M. Green. Hon. Alphonso Hart of the local committee of arrangements then made an address of welcome to the regiment in which he happily alluded to their well won laurels and bade them welcome in the name of the citizens of Ravenna and of Portage County. Gen. E. B. Tyler, the first Colonel of the Seventh was called for, and coming forward was greeted with hearty cheers. The General said the Seventh well knew he was not a speech maker, but still could not neglect the opportunity of greeting them publicly and expressing his great satisfaction in being with them on their anniversary day. The General alluded to some incidents of their army associations and in a familiar conversational manner entertained the audience for some moments. He alluded to the fact that seven years ago that day the Seventh Ohio was mustered into the service of the United States at Camp Taylor at Cleveland and briefly followed it down through [the] war. As he spoke of the noble and precious dead the hearts of all were touched with emotion and tears coursed down stern cheeks as these touching memories of the war were revived. At the conclusion of the General's remarks the association went into election of officers for the ensuing year. [The leadership was dominated by the men from the Cleveland area. The only local representative was Capt. S. S. Reed who was a member of the Executive Committee.]

A Constitution for the Association, prepared by a committee appointed a year ago was submitted, and after discussion adopted.

A report of the Regimental Monument was submitted to the effect that a contract for the monument had been entered into and that the same would be completed and dedicated at Cleveland on the 22d of November next.

At this point adjournment was had for dinner. Three tables had been spread in the lower Hall and were laden to the utmost with a most bountiful and luxuriant feast. In these dinner tables Ravenna did itself graceful honor. Nothing that could have added to the complete pleasure of this feature of the day had been omitted. It was a grand sight to see those citizen soldiers surrounded by wives and children and friends seated at the banquet and it was an occasion of compliment that they cannot well forget. Some sentiments were proposed and responded to by Gen. Tyler, Gen. Wm. Stedman, Rev. J. M. Green, Dr. J. G. Willis, Capt. DeForest, and others.

Afterwards the guests returned to their Hall and disposed of some unfinished business and listened to some impromptu remarks from individuals present...

[The resolutions were unanimously passed. They were mostly of a thank-you nature, such as the following:]

Resolved – That this meeting hereby return a vote of thanks to the Band who enlivened our stay by their fine music, to the boys who saluted us on our arrival with their gun and to all the Rail Roads who were so kind as to pass the members to the meeting on half fare.

Resolved: That in after years we shall ever mark this day as among the brightest of our lives and shall hold in cherished remembrance all who have contributed to our happiness. [20]

This reunion had been a celebration primarily for the living. Aside from the senior officers, they were still young men with prospects of a brighter future. However, from their past experiences they could agree with a quote from an article next to the newspaper report on the reunion. The writer of "Cemetery Matters" lamented the fickleness of the Grim Reaper, in particular the ages of his victims. The writer concluded that, "Surely, man is as the flower of the field. In the morning it flourisheth and groweth up, in the evening it is cut down and witherest." [21]

An expanded version of the above quote reads as follows:

Psalms 90.
    3. Thou turnest man to destruction; and sayest, Return ye children of men.
    4. For a thousand years in thy sight are but as yesterday when it is past, and as a watch in the night.
    5. Thou carriest them away as with a flood; they are as a sleep; in the morning they are like grass which groweth up.
    6. In the morning it flourisheth, and groweth up; in the evening it is cut down , and witherest...
    12. So teach us to number our days, that we may apply our hearts to wisdom.

If any of the soldiers of the Bully Seventh ever heard or read these verses, they might very well have whispered a reverent "Amen."

FOOTNOTES

Chapter One.

1. *Portage County Democrat*, (Ravenna, Ohio), "Letter From A Ravenna Printer Boy," June 26, 1861.
2. *Democrat*, "Letter From Camp Dennison," July 3, 1861.
3. *Democrat*, "Letter From A Ravennian In The Army," July 17, 1861.
4. *Democrat*, "Letter From Western Virginia," July 24, 1861.
5. *Democrat*, "Letters From The Army," August 7, 1861.
6. *Democrat*, "Letters From The Army," August 14, 1861.
7. *Democrat*, "Army Correspondence," August 21, 1861.
8. *Democrat*, "Army Correspondence," September 4, 1861.
9. *Ibid.*, The second letter of the article.
10. Sir William A. Craigie and James R. Hulbery, *A Dictionary of American English, Vol. II.* (Chicago: The University of Chicago Press, 1940), 962.
11. *The War Of The Rebellion, A Compilation of the Official Records of the Union and Confederate Armies, Series I, Vol. IV.* (Washington D.C.: Government Printing Office, 1893), 118-119; Vol. 51, Part I, Supplement, 459-463.
12. *Democrat*, "Army Correspondence," September 25, 1861.
13. *Democrat*, "Army Correspondence," October 9, 1861.
14. *Democrat*, "Col. E. B. Tyler – 7th Regiment," October, 2, 1861.
15. *Democrat*, "Army Correspondence," October 9, 1861.
16. *Democrat*, "Letter From The Army," October 23, 1861.
17. *Democrat*, "Army Letters From Western Virginia," December 11, 1861.
18. *Democrat*, Supplement, "Letter From Dr. I. Selby King," December 4, 1861.
19. *Democrat*, "Letter From The 7th Regiment," December, 18, 1861.
20. *Democrat*, Supplement, "Capt. F. A. Seymour..." December 4, 1861.
21. *Ibid.* Located under "Portage County ..."

Chapter Two

1. *Democrat*, "Army Letter," January 1, 1862.
2. Lawrence Wilson, *Itinerary of the Seventh Ohio Volunteer Infantry, 1861-1864* (New York and Washington: The Neale Publishing Company, 1907), 117.
3. *Democrat*, "From The 7th Regiment – The Victory At Blue Gap," January 29, 1862.
4. *Democrat*, "From The 7th Regiment – They Fall Back From Romney," January 29, 1862.
5. *Democrat*, "The Blue Gap Fight," January 22, 1862.
6. *Democrat*, "Withdrawal From Romney," January 22, 1862.
7. *Democrat*, "Army Letter From Virginia," February 5, 1862.
8. *Democrat*, Army Letter From Camp Kelly," February 5, 1862.
9. *Democrat*, "Letter From The 7th O.V.," February 19, 1862.
10. *Democrat*, "Army Letter From Virginia," February 26, 1862.
11. *Democrat*, "From The 7th O. V.," March 5, 1862.
12. *Democrat*, "Letter From The 7th O.V.," March 5, 1862.
13. *Democrat*, "Letter From Virginia." March 12, 1862.
14. *Democrat*, "Letter From Lieut. Reed,"March 19, 1862.
15. *Democrat*, "Col. Tyler's March," March 12, 1862.

Chapter Three

1. Frances H. Kennedy, *The Civil War Battlefield Guide* (Boston: Houghton Mifflin Company, 1990), 44. "The 1862 Shenandoah Valley Campaign," James I. Robertson.
2. *Ibid.*
3. *Democrat*, "Letter From Virginia, Battle of Winchester," April 9, 1862.
4. *Democrat*, "Col. E. B. Tyler," April 2, 1862.
5. *Democrat*, "The Winchester Battle!" April 2, 1862.
6. *Democrat*, "Camp Of The 7th Reg't. O. V. I.," April 9, 1862.
7. *Democrat*, "The Winchester Fight – Eleven members ..." April 2, 1862.
8. *Democrat*, "Letter From The 7th O. V.," April 16, 1862.
9. *Democrat*, "Letter From The 7th O. V.," May 7, 1862.
10. *Democrat*, "Letter From Shields' Division," May 7, 1862.
11. *Democrat*, "Letter From The 7th O. V.," May 14, 1862.
12. *Democrat*, April 30, 1862.

13. *Democrat*, "Correspondence Of The Portage County Democrat," May 21, 1862.
14. *Democrat*, "Picket Post Four Miles From Camp," May 28, 1862.
15. *Democrat*, "Letter From Virginia," June 4, 1862.
16. *Democrat*, "Murder Of Dr. I. S. King," June 4, 1862.
17. *Democrat*, "Killed and Wounded Of Co's F. and G.," June 18, 1862.

Chapter Four

1. *Democrat*, "From The Seventh," July 2, 1862.
2. *Democrat*, July 2, 1862.
3. *Democrat*, "How The Seventh Kept The Fourth," July 16 1862.
4. Wilson, *Itinerary, Vol. II.*, 593.
5. *Democrat*, "Camp Near Alexandria, Va.," August 6, 1862.
6. *Democrat*, "Letter From Virginia," August 20, 1862.
7. *Democrat*, "Daniel H. Wright, Jr., Dead," Aug. 20, 1862.
8. Wilson, *Itinerary*, 192.
9. *Democrat*, "Letter From Virginia," August 27, 1862.
10. *Democrat*, "Letter From Maryland," October 8, 1862.
11. Wilson, *Itinerary*, 593.
12. Stephen W. Sears, *Landscape Turned Red, The Battle Of Antietam* (New York: Warner Books, Inc., 1983), 256-257.
13. Frederick Tilberg, *Antietam*, (Washington, D.C.: Government Printing Office, 1960), 47.
14. *Democrat*, "Letter From Maryland," October 22, 1862.
15. *Democrat*, "The Bully Seventh," October 15, 1862.
16. *Democrat*, "Letter From Washington," October 29, 1862.
17. *Democrat*, "Mementoes of the Seventh," October 22, 1862.
18. *Western Reserve Chronicle* (Warren, Ohio), "From The Seventh Regiment," October 22, 1862.
19. *Democrat*, "Franklin," November 12, 1862.
20. *Democrat*, "How a Paroled Prisoner fared in Richmond," November 12. 1862.

Chapter Five

1. Kennedy, *Battlefield Guide*, 99-103. "Fredericksburg," by A. Wilson Green.

2. Maj. George L. Wood, *The Seventh Regiment: A Record* (New York: James Miller, 1865), 144-149.
3. Wood, *The Seventh Regiment*, gives the Union view of the battle at Dumfries. For the Confederate view, see Burke Davis, *Jeb Stuart, The Last Cavalier* (New York: Bonanza Books, 1957), 262.
4. *Democrat*, "Death Of Another Soldier," January 14, 1863.
5. *Democrat*, February 18, 1863.
6. *Ibid.*
7. *Western Reserve Chronicle*, "Letter From Lieut. Asper," March 25, 1863.
8. *Democrat*, March 11, 1863.
9. *Chronicle*, March 25, 1863.
10. *The Warren Constitution* (Warren, Ohio), "Who Are The Union Men," May 5, 1863.
11. *Ibid.*
12. Wood. The participation of the 7th Ohio at Chancellorsville is taken from this source. An excellent source for the entire battle is Stephen W. Sears' *Chancellorsville* (Boston: Houghton-Mifflin Company, 1996).
13. *Cleveland Morning Leader*, (Cleveland, Ohio), "From the 7th Ohio – The Part it bore in the Late Battle," May 15, 1863.
14. *Chronicle*, May 20 and 27, 1863.
15. Bruce Catton, *The Army of the Potomac: Glory Road* (Garden City, New York: Doubleday and Company, Inc., 1952), 228-233.
16. *Morning Leader*, May 28, 1863.
17. Bell Irvin Wiley, *The Life of Billy Yank* (Garden City, New York: Doubleday and Company, Inc., 1971), 64.
18. Catton, *Glory Road*, 233.
19. Glenn Tucker, *High Tide at Gettysburg* (Bobbs-Merrill Company, Inc., 1958, revised edition by Press of Morningside Bookshop, 1973), 72.
20. Jack McLaughlin, *Gettysburg The Long Encampment* (New York: Bonanza Books, 1963), 45.
21. Wilson, *Itinerary*, 248-260. The move from Acquia Creek to Gettysburg is based on Wilson's regimental history. The mileage, which is approximate, was found in several sources, including modern road maps. The 7th Ohio marched at least 104 miles from June 13 to July 1.
22. *Morning Leader*, July 15, 1863.
23. Wilson, 248-260 for the Gettysburg Campaign.

24. McLaughlin, 163-165.
25. *Morning Leader*, July 13, 1863.
26. Carl Sandburg, *Abraham Lincoln The War Years, Vol. II* (New York: Harcourt, Brace, & World, Inc., 1939), 344, 351.
27. *Report of the Committee to the Governor December 15, 1864.* The Morgan Raid Claims, 198. Ohio Historical Society Archives Library, Columbus, Ohio.
28. *Morning Leader*, July 13, 1863.
29. Kenneth W. Wheeler, *For The Union* (Columbus: The Ohio State University Press, 1968), 32.
30. Fred W. Almendinger, *An Historical Study of Holmes County, Ohio.* A thesis presented to the University of Southern California, Department of History, 1938. (Published by the Library Archives of Holmes County, Ohio, 1962), 87-90.
31. Rossiter Johnson, *Campfires and Battlefields* (New York: The Civil War Press, 1967), 284.
32. *Morning Leader*, July 13, 1863.
33. John S. Bowman, *The Civil War Almanac* (New York: Gallery Books, 1983), 162.
34. Johnson, 285-6.
35. *Morning Leader*, July 15, 1863.
36. Bowman, 162.
37. William Kepler, Ph.D., *4th Ohio Volunteers Gibraltar Brigade Army Of The Potomac* (Cleveland: Leader Printing Company, 1886; Reprinted by the Blue Alcorn Press, Huntington, W. Va., 1992), 210.
38. Wilson, 261.
39. Kepler, 141.
40. Wilson, 264.

Chapter Six

1. Wilson, *Itinerary*, 265-268. The Itinerary of the 7th Ohio's move from Bealton, Virginia to Wauhatchie.
2. *Official Records, Vol. 31. Part 2*, 700.
3. *Morning Leader*, October 15, 1863, 1.
4. U. S. Grant, *Personal Memoirs of U. S. Grant* (Cleveland and New York: The World Publishing Company, 1952), 317-318.
5. Grant, 319-320.
6. Grant, 335.
7. *Official Records, Vol. 33, Part 2*, 332.

8. *Ibid.*
9. *Ibid.* 333.
10. *Ibid.* 336.
11. Wilson, p. 283.
12. *Official Records, Vol. 33, Part 2*, 403-4.
13. *Ibid.* 407.
14. *Morning Leader*, December 7, 1863.
15. *Morning Leader*, December 1, 3, 4, 7, and 8, 1863. These issues extensively reported the deaths of Colonels Creighton and Crane, casualties in Company A, the funeral arrangements, and the funerals.
16. *Chronicle*, December 9, 1863.
17. *Morning Leader*, December 9, 1863.
18. *Official Records, Vol. 31, Part 2*, 410.
19. Wood, *A Record*, 166.
20. Wilson, 290.

Chapter Seven

1. Wilson, *Itinerary*, 290.
2. Wood, *A Record*, 196-97.
3. Wilson, 290-91.
4. *Morning Leader*, "From the Cumberland Army," April 12, 1864.
5. *Democrat*, March 30, 1864.
6. *Ibid*; also the *Bible*, Revelations, Chapter 6.
7. *Morning Leader*. February 5, 1864.
8. Wilson, 291-92.
9. *Morning Leader*. March 21, 1864.
10. Wilson, 293-94. Gen. Geary's report, which covered the same information is on 292-93.
11. Wilson, 295-96.
12. *Official Records, Vol. 38, Part 2*, 177-78. Lt. Col. Samuel McClellan's report of May 21, 1864.
13. Wilson, 296.
14. McClellan's report of May 21, 1864. See note # 12.
15. McClellan's report of June 9, 1864. 179-181.
16. Wilson, 311.
17. *Official Records, Vol. 38, Part 2*, 126. Gen. John Geary's report of September 15, 1864.
18. *Democrat*. June 29, 1864.

19. *Morning Leader*, June 28, 1864.
20. *Morning Leader*, June 25, 1864.
21. *Morning Leader*, June 27, 1864.
22. *Democrat*, June 29, 1864.
23. *Morning Leader*, July 8, 1864.
24. *Ibid.*
25. Wilson, 314.

Chapter Eight

1. Wilson, 360-61.
2. Walter Johnson Dickinson, *Pioneer History 1802-1865* (Ravenna, Ohio: Record Publishing Company, 1953), 94.
3. Richard A. Gabriel, *No More Heroes, Madness & Psychiatry In War* (New York: Hill and Wang, 1987), 57-58.
4. Mary Gardner Holland, *Our Army Nurses* (Roseville, Minnesota, Edinborough Press, 1998), 43-49 for the war service of Eunice Brown and 185-191 for the war service of Matilda Morris.
5. Gerald F. Lindeman, *Embattled Courage* (New York: The Free Press, 1987), 244.
6. *Ibid.* 247.
7. James M. McPherson, *For Cause and Comrades, Why Men Fought In The Civil War* (New York: Oxford University Press, 1997), 43.
8. Lindeman, 267.
9. Wilson, 361.
10. Earl J. Hess, *The Union Soldier In Battle, Enduring the Ordeal of Combat* (University Press of Kansas, 1997), 111, 114.
11. *Grand Army Blue Book 1895* (Philadelphia: J. B. Lippincott Company, 1896), 13-14.
12. *Democrat*, September 12, 1866.
13. *Democrat*, September 26, 1866.
14. *Democrat*, October 3, 1866.
15. *Democrat*, February 19, 1868.
16. *Democrat*, September 12, 1866.
17. *Ibid.*
18. Hess, 171.
19. *Democrat*, August 17, 1870.
20. *Democrat*, May 6, 1868.
21. *Ibid.*

BIBLIOGRAPHY

THE BULLY SEVENTH

Almendinger, Fred W. *An Historical Study of Holmes County, Ohio.* A thesis presented to the University of Southern California, Department of History, 1938. Published by the Library Archives of Holmes County, Ohio, 1962.

Bowman, John S. *The Civil War Almanac.* New York: Gallery Books, 1983.

Catton, Bruce. *The Army of the Potomac: Glory Road.* Garden City, New York: Doubleday and Company, Inc., 1952.

Craigie, Sir William A. and James R. Hulbery. *A Dictionary of American English, Vol. II.* Chicago: The University of Chicago Press, 1940.

Davis, Burke. *Jeb Stuart, The Last Cavalier.* New York: Bonanza Books, 1957.

Dickinson, Walter Johnson. *Pioneer History 1802-1865.* Ravenna, Ohio: Record Publishing Company, 1953.

Gabriel, Richard A. *No More Heroes, Madness & Psychiatry in War.* New York: Hill and Wang, 1987.

Grand Army Blue Book 1895. Philadelphia: J. B. Lippincott Company, 1896.

Grant, U. S. *Personal Memoirs of U. S. Grant.* Cleveland and New York: The World Publishing Company, 1952.

Hess, Earl J. *The Union Soldier In Battle, Enduring the Ordeal of Combat.* University Press of Kansas, 1997.

Holland, Mary Gardner. *Our Army Nurses.* Roseville, Minn.: Edinborough Press, 1998.

Johnson, Rossiter. *Campfires and Battlefields.* New York: The Civil War Press, 1967.

Kennedy, Frances H. *The Civil War Battlefield Guide.* Boston: Houghton Mifflin Company, 1990.

Kepler, William, Ph.D. *4th Ohio Volunteers Gibraltar Brigade Army Of The Potomac.* Cleveland" Leader Printing Company, 1886; Reprinted by the Blue Acorn Press, Huntington, W. Va., 1992.

Lindeman, Gerald F. *Embattled Courage*. New York: The Free Press, 1987.

McLaughlin, Jack. *The Long Encampment*. New York: Bonanza Books, 1963.

McPherson, James M. *For Cause and Comrades, Why Men Fought In The Civil War*. New York: Oxford University Press, 1997.

Official Roster of the Soldiers Of The State Of Ohio in the War Of The Rebellion, 1861-1866. Cincinnati: The Ohio Valley Pub. & Mfg. Co., 1886.

Report of the Committee to the Governor December 15, 1864. The Morgan Raid Claims. Ohio Historical Society, Archives Library.

Sandburg, Carl. *Abraham Lincoln The War Years, Vol. II*. New York: Harcourt, Brace & World, Inc., 1939.

Sears, Stephen W. *Landscape Turned Red, The Battle Of Antietam*. New York: Warner Books, Inc., 1983.

Tilberg, Frederick. *Antietam*. Washington: Government Printing Office, 1960.

Tucker, Glen. *High Tide at Gettysburg*. Bobbs-Merrill Company, Inc., 1958, revised edition by Press of Morningside Bookshop, 1973.

The War Of The Rebellion: A Compilation Of The Official Records Of The Union And Confederate Armies. Washington: Government Printing Office, 1893.

Wheeler, Kenneth W. *For The Union*. Columbus: The Ohio State University Press, 1968.

Wiley, Bell Irvin. *The Life of Billy Yank*. Garden City, New York: Doubleday and Company, Inc., 1971

Wilson, Lawrence. *Itinerary of the Seventh Ohio Volunteer Infantry, 1861-1864*. New York and Washington: The Neale Publishing Company, 1907.

Wood, Maj. George L. *The Seventh Regiment: A Record*. New York: James Miller, 1865.

NEWSPAPERS

Cleveland Morning Leader. Cleveland, Ohio.
Portage County Democrat. Ravenna, Ohio.
Western Reserve Chronicle. Warren, Ohio.
Warren Constitution. Warren, Ohio.

INDEX

ABOLITIONISM, opinions on 104
ADAMS, Pvt. Arthur 81
Adams, Cpl. Theron 7
ARMY ROUTINE, 58-60
ARTILLERY Units, Daum's Battery 34 35 42, 63 Knapp's Battery 106
ASHBY, Col. Turner 45 55 62
Asper, Capt. J. F. 6 48 50 86 101 109
ATWATER, E. B. 93
AUXER, Pvt. Jas. B. 141
BACON, (Bascom) Pvt. Henry 95
BACON, J. 151
BANKS, Gen. N. P. 46 47 76 79
BAPTIST, (Baptie), John 131
BARBER, Henry O. 151
BARNARD, Pvt. Clark E. 51
BARNUM, Pvt. Saml. H. 108 109 Robt. M. Miller 109
BARRETT, Capt. 109
BARRETT, Sgt. Geo. W. 51 81 85
BATTLES, Blue Gap 30 31, Cross Lanes 11-16 93, Romney 33 34, Winches-

BATTLES (continued) ter 45-52 93 96 Port Republic 66-68 83 93 96 Cedar Mt. 79-82 85 92 93 96 South Mt. 87 88 Antietam 84 88-96 Dumphries 99 Fredericksburg 99 Chancelloresville 106-109 Gettysburg 112-116 Chattanooga 123-128 134 Ringgold 128-134 142 Atlanta Campaign 141-147
BAXTER, Adj. Morris 131
BEERY, Lyman 151
BELLOWS, Surg. Curtis J. 152
BERTHOLF, Pvt. Gilbert D. 51 81 85
BETHEL, Fred 52
BOND, Pvt. Wm. R. 51
BOWLER, Sgt. Chas. P. 73
BOYNTON, Mrs. Mercia 109
BRADEN, Capt. W. J. 131 151
BRAGG, Gen. Braxton 123 126
BRISBANE, Lt. Jas. P. 80
BROWN, Eunice 158
BROWN, Ezra 81
BROWN, Rev. Fred. T. 11 13
BROWN, John 92
BROWN, Sgt. Thos. C. 13
BROUGH, Gov. John 124 150 151
BRYON, Pvt. Jas. C. 51
BUCKLEY, Col. 86
BULL, Cpl. Austin 51 99 100

BURGESS, Capt. 48 52
BURNSIDE, Gen. Ambrose
    91 96 103 110
BURT, Cpl. M. V. 67 151
BUTLER, Pvt. A. R. 22
BUTLER, S. F. (CSA) 93
BUTTERFIELD, Gen. Danl.
    126
CADWELL, G. M. 81
CALLOW, Cpl. Wm. T.
    51 81
CAMP DENNISON, v vi 1 3
CAMP TAYLOR, Cleveland
    vi Virginia 4
CANDY, Col. Chas. 116
CARL, Pvt. Geo. K. 51
CARL, Geo. R. 68
CARRIN, G. W. 81
CARROLL, Gen. 75
CARTER, Col. H. L. 52
CARTER, Sgt. J. B. 81 90
    91 95
CASE, H. C. 81
CASEMATE, Maj. John S.
    2 16 17 31 47 50
CAVANAH, Capt. A. A. 149
    150
CHAPMAN, Leroy M. 67
CHENEY, Pvt. Chas. H. 107
CLARK, Lt. Col. 103
CLARK, L. J. 66
CLARK, N. D. 94
CLAYTON, D. B. 3 14
CLEBURNE, Gen. Pat. 128
COE, Allison 92
CONNECTICUT, 5th Inf. 48
COPPERHEAD MOVE-
    MENT, 102 103 110 118
    121 124
COTTER, Capt. Chas. S. 27

COX, Gen. Jacob D. 4 12-16 18
    26 86 87
CRAIG, Cpl. John D. 108
CRANE, Lt. Col. Orrin J. 19 84
    86 103 124 128-133 136 152
CREIGHTON, Col. Wm. R. 2 31
    47 50 67 74 80 81 103 110 111
    128-133 136 152
CROMWELL, Pvt. Wm. 51
CROSS, Lt. Judson N. 19 139
DANFORTH, Sgt. 48
DAVIS, Lt. L. R. 78 136
DAWES, Pvt. John W. 104-106
DAY, Lt. A. H. 67 85
DEAN, Lt. Harry M. 51 68 137
DEFOREST, Adj. Louis G. 36
    43 167
DELONG, Cpl. Cyrus 68
DICKINSON, Walter J. 156
DINGES, Pvt. Henry F. 81
DOUTHETT, Cpl. John H. 81
DOWNER, Pvt. John 81
DRAFT RIOTS, 119-122
DRAKE, Rev. 11
DYER, Capt. John 15 20 21
    41 wife 20
EARLY, Gen. Jubal 155
EATINGER, Pvt. Sherman 81
EATON, Lt. Henry Z. 50
EILEMAN, Prof. 8 44
ELDRIDGE, Sgt. Frank 68 74
ELY, Pvt. Thomas 81
EWELL, Gen. Richard S. 66
    80 114
EXECUTIONS, 112
F.F.V.'s, 14
FISHER, Pvt. Saml. S. 51
FLOYD, Gen. John B. 11 12 18
    20 23 25 37 40
FRAM, Pvt. John 48 51

FULLER, S. A. 81 85
FURRY, Cpl. Geo. A. 51 151
G.A.R., 160 163
GARFIELD, Gen. Jas. A. 27 36 162
GEARY, Gen. John 80 85 92 111-113 116 123 125-130 140-146
GEYLIN, Pvt. Geo. O. 68
GIBBONS, Wm. 85
GILLIS, Chas. 27
GRANNIS, Att. J. C. 150
GRANT, Gen. U. S. 125 126 140 163
GREEN, Pvt. Isaiah B. 51 81
GREEN, Rev. J. M. 166 167
GREENE, Gen. Geo. S. 84 88 89 90 91
GRIDLEY, Cpl. Benj. 19 81 96 David 96 Wm. 97 98
GRINNELL, Pvt. Oliver 131
GUITCHELL, Nathaniel 81
HALL, Elias 52
HALLECK, Gen. H. W. 112
HANDSOM, John 81
HANSEN, Horatio 68
HARMON, Q.M. Sgt. Frank 137
HARSH, Pvt. Franklin 51
HART, Hon. Alphonso 166
Hazen, Col. Wm. B. 27 125
HERRICK, Ira 68
HICKOX, Chauncey 27
HILL, Adj. Gen. 139
HITCHCOCK, Asst. Surg. E. 100

HOLCOMBE, Pvt. Jarvin M. 81
HOLMES COUNTY, OHIO uprising 118 119
HOLTON, H. M. 68 84
HOOKER, Gen. Joseph 103 106 112 123 127 131 140 144 145
HOOVER, Marion 68 74
HOPKINS, Lt. Marcus 81
HOPKINS, Pvt. Stephen A. 81
HORTON, Pvt. Marcus C. 72
HOUCK, Pvt. Geo. W. 51
HOWARD, Pvt. Henry 51 81
HOWARD, Gen. O. O. 123
HUBBARD, Sgt. Newton K. 146
HUDSON, Pvt. Austin 51
HUGHES, Pvt. Morris R. 51
HUGHES, Pvt. Tod 68
HUMMEL, Chas. 24
HUNTER, Pvt. Wm. 109
ILLINOIS, 68TH Inf. 75
INDIANA, regiments of 6th Inf. 2 7th Inf. 2 30 34 35 42 14th Inf. 30 32 33rd Inf. 124
JACKSON, Andrew 161
JACKSON, Gen. Thos. J. 45 57 79 80 106
JOHNSON, Pres. Andrew 161
JOHNSON, Gen. Edw. 114
JOHNSON, Lt. Frank 80
JOHNSON, Pvt. Wm. H. 68 131
JOHNSTON, Gen. Jos. 146 155
JONES, Pvt. Daniel 81
KIMBALL, Lt. Dudley A. 14
KINCAID, Jos. 96
KING, Sgt. Chas. L. 51 68 74
KING, Dr, Ira Selby 24 25 66 137 Carrie 66 Georgie 66 Gen. John. B. 66
KRIEGER, Capt. Ernst J. 131 135
LANDER, Gen. Fred. W. 34 38

LANDER, (continued) 39 41
  42 45
LAWTERWASSER, Sgt.
  Wm. 50
LAZARUS, Sgt. Edw. M. 48
  51 81 85 151
LAZURUS, Pvt. Martin 51
  90 91 95
LECOMPTE, Sgt. Theodore 11
LEE, Gen. Robt. E. 99 116
  123
LENTZ, John 96
LEWIS, Boynton 68
LINCOLN, Pres. A. 92 112
  117
LINDEMAN, Gerald F. 158
  159
LONGSTREET, Gen. Jas.
  111 112 114 123
LOOMIS, P. D. 81
LOOMIS, A.Q.M. Stephen
  T. 136
LOUCKS, (Laucks) Sgt.
  Jas. R. 51 68 74 83 84
MANSFIELD, Gen. Jos.
  K. F. 84 88 91
MATHEWS, David 81
MATTHEWS, Sylvester 68
  81
MAY, Pvt. Alfred E. 51 151
McCLELLAN, Gen. Geo. B.
  1 8 16 58 74 84 88 91
McCLELLAN, Col. Saml. 50
  109 141 144 146 147 149
  150 166
McDOWELL, Gen. Irvin 58
  63
McFARLAND, Pvt. Jas. 151
McKAY, Lt. Geo. 136

McLAIN, (McCain) Pvt. Willis F.
  19
McPHERSON, Jas. M. 158
MEACHAM, Elbridge F. 95
MEADE, Gen. Geo. G. 112 116
  116
MERRILL, Pvt. Benton 68
MERRILL, Pvt. J. H. 114 115
  132 uncle J.M. Stull 113
MINARD, Pvt. Milo 81 85
MINNICK, Pvt. Chas. W. 52
MISSISSIPPI, 11th Inf. 93
MOLYNEAUX, Adj. Jos. B.
  49 50 81
MOODY, Col. 55
MORELEY, Pvt. Alfred W. 68
MORGAN, Gen. John H. 117
  118
MORRIS, Matilda 158
MURRAY, Col. 84th Pa. 48
NESPER, Lt. Christian W. 137 138
NEAPER, Capt. Geo. 136
NEW HAMPSHIRE, 7th Inf. 48 49
NEW YORK, 66th Inf. (typo?) 99
  69th Inf. 75
NICHOLSON, A. 151
NITSCHEIM, Lt. C. F. 12
NORTHROP, Sgt. Eli 151
NUNEMAKER, D. C. 81
O'BRIAN, Capt. 39-41
OHIO, 1st Cav. 39 3rd Inf. 3 4th Inf.
  3 30 32 122 5th Inf. 30 32 34 73
  86 99 106 107 110 111 145 146
  165 6th Cav. 27 105 6th Inf. 32
  8th Inf. 30 32 9th Inf. 1 10th Inf.
  2 13th Inf. 2 9 17th Inf. 9 19th Inf.
  109 29th Inf. 35 42 73 86 103 116
  142 165 41st Inf. 27 145 42nd Inf.
  27 66th Inf. 42 55 73 86 103 115
  116 124 103rd Inf. 78 104th Inf.

OHIO, (continued)
161 Cleveland Light
Guards 3, Franklin Rifles
vi 51 155, Tyler Guards vi,
99 155
ORVIS, Pvt. Recellus W. 21
151
OVIATT, J. F. 81
OWEN, Pvt. Humphrey 51
151
OWEN, Lewis 81 85
OWEN, Moses 52
PARKER, Wm. 117 118
Daniel 117 118
PENNSYLVANIA, Ringold
Cav. 30 34 35 37 42, 10th
34, 28th 86 88 110th 35 42
147th Inf. 143
PERRY, Wm. 151
PIDGIN, Pvt. Jas. 51
POOR, Pvt. Wm. H. 141
POPE, Gen. John 76 77 78
80 85 86 94
POTTS, Pvt. Israel 151
POWELL, Lt. Col. 103
PRISONS, Richmond 83 84
97 98
PRITCHARD, Anson 52
QUAY, Capt. E. S. 36 47
49 67 72
RHODE Island, 1st Cav. 105
REED, Cpl. Loren 81 151
REED, Lt. S. S. 36 44 50 61
81 85 101 162 167
REMEL, Lawrence 67
RENO, Gen. Jesse L. 87
REUNIONS, 163-168
REYNOLDS, V. 151
RHODENBAUGH, Mr.
John 100

RIPPLE, Pvt. Wm. H. 51 151
RISK, Cpl. R. M. 81
ROBINSON, Lt. W. Henry 22
ROGERS, Wm. W. (R.) 68
ROSECRANS,, Gen. Wm. S.
15-19 26 123 125
ROSS, Lt. Jos. H. 80
RUOFF, Cpl. Julius 68
RUSSELL, Pvt. Gideon T. 52
SALTER, Surg. Francis 66
SCHUTTE, Capt. John T. 13 14
SENFERT, Pvt. Wm. 108
SEYMOUR, Maj. Fred. A. 14 26
53 63 84 92 95 135 136 165
SEYMOUR, Gov. Horatio 121
SHAW, Pvt. Stacey (Stanley) 151
SHERMAN, Gen. Wm. T. 126 140
142 144 145
SHIELDS, Gen. Jas. 45 53 56
SHIRTLIFF, Capt. Giles W. 7 8
SKINNER, Mrs. M. B. 24
SLOCUM, Gen. Henry W. 123
SMITH, "Extra Billy" 65
SMITH, Pvt. Philip 51
SMITH, Gen. Wm. F. 125
SMITH, Pvt. Zenas K. 51
SPARR, Rev. Capt. 12
SPENCER, Lt. H. A. 131 136
SPRAGUE, Capt. John W. 14 38
SPRINGER, Mrs. T. G. 56
STEADMAN, Pvt. Albert 68
STEDMAN, Pvt. Arthur C. 51
STEDMAN, Wm. 3 27 161 167
STEIN, Pvt. David G. 3 35 40 43
54 56 58 74 80 82 94
STERLING, Capt. Jas. T. 17 31
32 50 78 81
STONEMAN, Gen. Geo. 105
STRATTON, Sgt. Isaac 131
STRONG, Frank 81 85

STUART, Gen. Jeb 99 106
TAYLOR, Sgt. E. G. 81
TAYLOR, Gen. Richard 66
THOMAS, Gen. Geo. 123 126
THOMPSON, Edw. 52
TISDEL, Sgt. Maj. W. P 130
TOD, Gov. David 119
TRACY, E. E. 52
TREMBLEY, Sgt. Oliver 147 148
TWITCHELL, Arby 52
TYLER, Gen. E. B. 1-3 6 9-11 15 16 19-21 27 31 33 34 36 37 42 43 44 47 49 50 56 66 67 73 75 77 80 85 94 102 110 111 163 164 166 167
TYNDALE, Lt. Col. Hector 84 86 88 90
VALLANDIGHAM, Clement 102 110 112 118 124
VETERAN CONVENTIONS, 160-163
VIRGINIA, Wise's Brigade 9 10, Capt, White's Guerilla Band 62
WAIGHT, Hiram 81
WALKER, S. P. (Waller) 81 85
WALLACE, Col. Wm. 119
WASHINGTON'S BIRTHDAY, celebration of 41-43
WEBB, Sgt-Maj. 48
WEST VIRGINIA, Kelly Lancers 30, Snake Hunters 9 12 13, 1st 30 32 34 35 42, 1st Cav. 39, 7th 32

WHITMORE, Pvt. Thos. H. 51 81 85
WICKS, Pvt. Jerry 51
WILCOX, Lt. Arthur T. 17
WILLIAMSON, Lt. 29th Ohio 48
WILLIS, Capt. J. G. 72 167
WILSON, Sgt. Lawrence 107 134-136 142 153
WINTERSTEEN, Cpl. David 109
WINZENRIED, Pvt. Ralph 81
WISE, Gov. Henry A. 14
WOOD, Maj. Geo. L. 134 135
WOODARD, Drum Maj. Joshua I. 36
WOOLF, Pvt. Adam 51
WOOLF, Pvt. Thos. 51
WRIGHT, Cpl. Daniel H. 9 11 25 36 38 45 49 51 53 61 63 65 69 72 75 78-81 85
WRIGHT, Chap. D. C. 73 78

Other Heritage Books by Richard J. Staats:

*A Grassroots History of Baseball:
Days of the Rosewood Bat and the Silver Ball*

*A Grassroots History of the American Civil War, Volume I:
The Life and Times of Pvt. Ephraim Cooper,
One of Mr. Lincoln's First Volunteers*

*A Grassroots History of the American Civil War, Volume II:
The Bully Seventh Ohio Volunteer Infantry*

*A Grassroots History of the American Civil War, Volume III:
Captain Cotter's Battery*

*A Grassroots History of the American Civil War, Volume IV:
The Life and Times of Colonel William Stedman of the 6th Ohio Cavalry*

A Grassroots History of World War II: Eight Men in Granite

*The History of the Sixth Ohio Volunteer Cavalry, 1861-1865:
A Journal of Patriotism, Duty and Bravery*

www.ingramcontent.com/pod-product-compliance
Lightning Source LLC
Chambersburg PA
CBHW072128160426
43197CB00012B/2037